THE DEARS
lost in the plot

THE DEARS

LORRAINE CARPENTER

Invisible Publishing
Halifax & Toronto

Library and Archives Canada Cataloguing in Publication

Carpenter, Lorraine
          The Dears : lost in the plot / Lorraine Carpenter.

(Bibliophonic ; 1)
ISBN 978-1-926743-13-4

          1. Dears (Musical group). 2. Rock musicians--Canada--
Biography. I. Title. II. Series: Bibliophonic ; 1

ML421.D285C29 2011   782.42166092   C2011-901671-0

Cover photo by Francesca Tallone | www.patternclash.com
Interior designed by Megan Fildes

Typeset in Laurentian by Megan Fildes
With thanks to type designer Rod McDonald

Printed and bound in Canada

Invisible Publishing
Halifax & Toronto
www.invisiblepublishing.com

We acknowledge the support of the Canada Council for the Arts which last year invested $20.1 million in writing and publishing throughout Canada.

Invisible Publishing recognizes the support of the Province of Nova Scotia through the Department of Communities, Culture & Heritage. We are pleased to work in partnership with the Culture Division to develop and promote our cultural resources for all Nova Scotians.

NOVA SCOTIA
Communities, Culture and Heritage

Canada Council
for the Arts

Conseil des Arts
du Canada

FULL DISCLOSURE
PREFACE

I WAS 16 WHEN I MOVED INTO THE MASTER BEDROOM in my parents' apartment, a room previously inhabited by my older brother, and my older sister before him. I vividly remember watching the video for "How Soon Is Now" by The Smiths the night my family moved into the top floor of that triplex in 1985. But not much Smiths was played on the turntable there; my musical education was dominated by my siblings' records, mostly David Bowie, The Beatles, Roxy Music and The Velvet Underground, along with a range of questionable '80s bands[1].

It was only in the '90s, when I was a Suede fanatic, that I truly became enamoured with The Smiths. And in that bedroom (in a beautiful old building, incidentally[2]) I heard

---

[1] My first concert, at age nine, was The Thompson Twins.
[2] Gratuitous Smiths reference #1: "Paint a Vulgar Picture".

The Smiths not only on my stereo, but through the wall.

It was shocking to me then that someone else, someone right next door, was listening to this vaguely gay, English '80s band in the era of Pearl Jam. I know now that I was hardly alone, as young Britpop fans everywhere had found The Smiths the way I had, just as teenagers in the aughts took the cue from emo idols like My Chemical Romance or Fallout Boy (I've seen the homemade Smiths t-shirts to prove it). Even on that one block in Montreal, there was a kindred spirit. Years later, I found out that that person was Murray Lightburn.

I first knew Murray as the one black guy at all the Britpop concerts. We met behind the recently demolished Spectrum, where we were both stalking some band or another after a show. He chatted to a friend of mine, who was then a VJ on MusiquePlus (Quebec's MuchMusic), about a band he'd put together called The Dears.

Our first real conversation happened years later, with our first interview in April of 2000. A colleague and I met members of four local bands at Bar Miami, on Montreal's St-Laurent blvd., for a large article in our university newspaper, *The Concordian*. Murray spoke about modelling his career after that of Serge Gainsbourg, who released his first album at 30 (Murray was then 29) and The Smiths, who put out five albums in as many years ("If you do it like The Smiths and achieve Morrissey status after, that's all you need, forget about it"). I described The Dears' music as "dramatic tales of urban angst and lost love sitting atop touchy-feely classic pop."

The four bands played McGill University's CKUT benefit

show at Jailhouse Rock Café the week that piece was published. Unfortunately, my only memory of that show, my first exposure to The Dears, resembled a scene out of a horrible high school drama: I saw Natalia flirting with a guy I had a crush on. Or at least that's how it appeared at the time. "That bitch," my friend said.

Somehow, Murray and I became friends. Somehow, I ended up as an extra in the video for "End of a Hollywood Bedtime Story," a role I recently reprised in the video for "Omega Dog[3]." In the intervening years, Murray and Natalia and I have occasionally broken bread and gone to movies together; Murray has counselled me in times of boy trouble; I've attended a few of Neptune's epic birthday parties.

But all the while, I kept writing about The Dears, for the *Montreal Mirror, Exclaim, Chart* and *Under the Radar*. Anglo Montreal is such a small town that no editor has ever accused me of being biased[4]. It's as normal for local writers to know their subject personally or professionally, or at least be separated by very few degrees, as it is for my conversations with Murray to shift in and out of interview mode, on and off the record. That's how our friendship began.

Knowing Murray and Natalia, and being acquainted with all the other Dears, has helped me put this book together; if anything has hindered my objectivity, it's not those relationships, but the fact that I'm a longtime, diehard fan. What differentiates this book from the series of articles I've written about the band over the years is the level of detail,

---

3 You actually see me this time, near the end, in a red beret.
4 One of those editors was my boyfriend for seven years, the same guy I thought I saw Natalia flirting with. How's that for conflict of interest?

analysis and criticism. I've now picked apart every last Dears record in depth. (Hopefully, after they've read this, Murray and Natalia will have me back for dinner.)

We now live in the same neighbourhood. My apartment is located on the very avenue, but fortunately not the block, that inspired Murray and Natalia to coin the term "degeneration street." You could call it "ghetto." And with walls as thin as ever, I still lay in awe on my bedroom floor[5], listening to The Dears.

---

5 Gratuitous Smiths reference #2: " Rubber Ring".

INTRODUCTION

OF COURSE MONTREAL IS UNIQUE. It's the urban centre of a French province on an English and Spanish continent, with all the quirks, wonders and troubles that such a politically tense and culturally fruitful juxtaposition brings. But in many ways, Montreal is also a typical North American city: a piece of land (an island) that was founded, settled and developed by conquerors and immigrants, one that's famous for cultural touchstones that have flourished here, but originated in our old countries, sometimes by way of the superpower to the south[6].

In the late '70s, the rise of nationalist fervour inspired a slow exodus of English-speaking (anglo) Montrealers that

---

6 U.S. is Canada's primary trading partner, not just in goods and services, but in culture. We give them great comedians and overrated film directors. They give us everything they have to offer, usually without stepping across the border. From the trash to the treasure, it seeps in, through the TV, radio, Internet, food and water. Luckily we're not completely gun-crazy. But we can sure shoot up a school.

would last for two decades. But once the threat of separation from Canada subsided, taking the recession down with it, not only did native anglos stay put, but a segment of the steady influx of students from other provinces and countries began to plant roots. Some of them formed bands, founded festivals or otherwise created and hustled to enrich the local art scene.

English musicians from these parts used to take their quest for a career to Toronto, the national hub of the music industry. Now, it's not uncommon to hear about bands relocating from their city to Montreal, to tap into the storied recording studios, live venues, hipster hangouts and cheap rents that fed the successes of the mid-aughts.

That scene remains small, and with 68 percent of the city being francophone, Québécois culture looms large. But despite this, the past decade has given us a pack of anglo bands and a scene to be proud of [7], to the particular delight of pop music connoisseurs and indie-label patrons.

As the old music industry declined, locally grown bands ascended, elevated largely by grassroots enthusiasm and a media groundswell. In particular, there was one Montreal band, with a husband and wife at its core, with too many

---

7 One that's full of francophone musicians and the occasional French-language band that crosses over, Malajube and Karkwa being prime examples. Ironically, bands such as those, and Pas Chic Chic, Les Breastfeeders and the defunct Les Georges Leningrad, appeal to anglos not because they mimic that anglo-Canadian chamber pop sound (and there are some who do), but because they don't play fiddles or accordions (or sing about nationalism), as many Québécois bands do (even the "alternative"ones), drawing on a tradition derived from Celtic music. A lot of franco acts also reflect what have traditionally been the most popular genres in this province: reggae, classic/progressive rock and house. In other words, the majority of Québécois music is to hipsters as garlic is to vampires.

people on stage, playing guitars, drums, strings, brass, synths, organs and pianos, their music and lyrics sometimes steeped in malaise and melancholia, sometimes buoyed by anthemic power, evoking the apocalypse, invoking Christianity, losing their sweat and lifting your spirits on stages across the city, around the world, sometimes even at your local church.

Ladies and gentlemen: The Dears.

––––––––

"Something that was a curse to us was being slightly ahead of the curve," says Dears singer Murray Lightburn, looking back on his band's first decade. "I found that to be the case with a lot of Montreal bands," he adds, citing '90s garage rockers Tricky Woo, "that they have this sound, and then five years later, someone else makes it famous."

Before The Dears released *End of a Hollywood Bedtime Story* in 2000, "orchestral pop noir romantique" didn't exist in North America[8]. Five years later, brass and string sections were ubiquitous, and it was no accident. Both Arcade Fire and Broken Social Scene opened for The Dears in 2003 (before releasing their breakthrough albums[9]), both having been admirers since the early days[10].

To paraphrase Kim Cook, the Canadian record company

––

8 Even overseas, bands with similar instrumentation and common influences, like Belle and Sebastian, made music with a very different flavour, under the influence of vintage British folk and peppy American pop.

9 Stateside in the case of BSS, whose *You Forgot It in People* came out in Canada in late 2002.

10 In 2000, the year he arrived in Montreal, Win Butler was "cyber-stalking" the band, according to Lightburn, insisting that he meet them in person, at the home of Natalia Yanchak, to present a cassette of his music. "It creeped me out," says Yanchak, who referred him to their label's P.O. Box. He never sent the demo.

man who signed The Dears twice, The Dears laid out the buffet—serving heaping helpings of what Lightburn describes as "sweeping, inclusive, orchestral, left field pop music"—and everybody showed up and ate.

"We laid down stone for an entire scene in this country, yet no one ever mentions that we were the band that put this path in place," Lightburn says, bemoaning the band's exclusion from media reports and best-of lists. "I know how that sounds. People might read that and say, 'What an asshole.' But if you actually look at what came out in 2000 and what happened in its wake and our relationship with these bands, you can see it right there."

It's true. And The Dears are as good a band as any Canadian act of the aughts. But why didn't they get the glory? Being "ahead of the curve," as Lightburn said, or simply victims of bad timing, is as good a reason as any. The hype behind the band, particularly in North America, peaked just prior to the rise of social media and blogs, before online trumpeting could propel a band as far as it can today. Perhaps that's why, when the Montreal scene was being feted in a succession of major publications, their name was usually absent—the only organization to shine the spotlight on The Dears in a Montreal-scene piece was CBC's *The National*, Canada's nightly news show.

The impact of business dealings on a band's image, and the perception of momentum or decline, can (sadly) propel a band's rise, fall or coast. In those crucial early years, The Dears were never signed to a hip label, while Arcade Fire and the now defunct Wolf Parade were snapped up by Merge and Sub Pop—without these signings, a lot less ink would've been spilled over the "Montreal scene." And during that other crucial period, the creation, execution and aftermath of *Gang of Losers*, from 2005–2008, the band's near-implosion left them bruised, inspiring a series of bluesy interviews and even bluesier songs. It's as if their doomsday fantasies were a self-fulfilling prophecy.

There are, of course, other factors. I could theorize about race. Or the Britpop tag. Or the Morrissey curse. But some of the same grandiose musical aesthetics, large-looming influences, heart-on-sleeve lyrics and interviews and vaguely obnoxious rock star vibes that arguably keep The Dears off the charts are the very elements that have fuelled their critical acclaim, and cult following[11]. No one wants a tamer, more homogenous Dears. And judging by their latest album, we're not going to get one.

The Dears have proven themselves. Depending on their luck, longevity and drive to, as Lightburn put it, "harness the power of the universe," their future could be as bright as parts of their past have been dark. It's true that The Dears have been celebrated in some circles, yet the kind of global ovation that a hungry young band craves has probably passed them by. But it's high time for credit, and that—along with telling a captivating, largely untold story and examining a wealth of inspiring, exciting and moving songs—is what this book hopes to achieve.

Pour la passion,
Lorraine Carpenter

---

11 As well as their appearance, for nine consecutive years, on the *Montreal Mirror*'s Most Pretentious Band list, as voted by readers.

CHAPTER 1
He is just so fanatical

"You're a teenager, you just wanna fuckin'
bang your head up against the wall.
Being a suburban kid, [music] was an escape."

BORN TO A JAZZ MUSICIAN AND A NURSE, Murray Lightburn
went to his first gigs as a toddler, sometimes sleeping in the
back rooms of nightclubs while his father played on stage.
After his parents became born-again Christians, his father
putting down the sax to take up the cloth as a Pentecostal
minister, Lightburn and his three older brothers were
forbidden to see movies or watch TV. Well, most TV. "The
rise of TV/celebrity evangelism like PTL, Jimmy Swaggart,
Oral Roberts and shit like that is directly responsible for my
utterly miserable childhood," Lightburn says.

Music was his salvation. Hymns, gospel, '70s R&B and
"cheesy" jazz records were on regular rotation, as was the
proto-hip hop and '80s pop brought home by his brothers.
When he was 15, his brother Peter, who would become a DJ
and house music aficionado, introduced him to what was

then called college rock. With one listen to *U2 Live at Red Rocks: Under a Blood Red Sky*, he was radicalized.

He'd already fiddled with drums, cello and sax, but when he found a guitar with no strings in his parents' basement, he taught himself to play.

Coming home to the guitar and a new world of music got him through the day at Centennial Regional High School in Greenfield Park; the neighbourhood next to his, Brossard, on Montreal's South Shore. He drifted from clique to clique, getting along with everyone but fitting in with no one. When he started singing to himself at his locker one day, he attracted the attention of a "preppie jock" who'd once briefly bullied him, until Lightburn shoved him into a wall—then they became friends.

"So he came up to me and said, 'Hey, you sound like this guy Morrissey—do you ever listen to The Smiths?'" Lightburn said no, and went home that day with a borrowed copy of *Hatful of Hollow*. "I put on the tape and started freaking out, like, what the fuck is this? It spoke to me a lot—what he was saying was a big deal. It was what music is supposed to do, to me anyway.

"I brought my friend Andrew [White] over and played him this cassette and made him a copy. That was all we listened to for at least a year."

Lightburn and White learned to play guitar and bass to a number of rock records (including The Cult's *Electric*), but The Smiths was the main inspiration for their first band, The Sacred Wunderkind, a moniker lifted from a Smiths song, "These Things Take Time". With Lightburn on vocals and guitar, White on bass and Brett Watson on drums (he later became an actor, playing Def Leppard's first drummer in a biopic), they played a handful of shows at long-gone Montreal venues like Station 10. It wasn't until the dawn of the '90s, when they got a new drummer, an additional guitarist and new name, Wren, that they began to attract attention. Described as "a four-piece band of angry young men in sharp suits with a mesmerizingly heroic lead singer," the band tried to reconcile classic pop tropes and math rock rhythms, flirting with unconventional time signatures and other staples of the period's more angular alternative rock. But it wasn't built to last.

"We didn't really know what we were doing. We just put all of our faith and any money we had into this band. We were in complete financial dire straits and it just fell apart."

But not completely. Lightburn briefly formed a duo with Wren's drummer John Tod, called Tidal Wave.

"It was really, really weird. It was just instrumental, kind of surfy, kind of garagey, kind of punky, kind of poppy."

Left out on the sidelines, White wanted in. A new band was in the making, with White on bass, but Lightburn was unsure of what role he himself would play.

"I was thinking of hanging up my vocal chords and just being the guitar player. I wanted to focus on one thing and be good at one thing. So we went about trying to find a singer. We tried a couple of girls and then we tried a couple of dudes, and each audition ended with the person saying, 'Why aren't you singing?'"

With Lightburn returning to centre stage, the band sought out another guitarist, eventually settling on Richard MacDonald. Inspired by Lightburn's latest batch of rich, romantic and relatively accessible tunes, White named the band The Dears.

––––––––

Meanwhile, across the provincial border in Toronto, Natalia Yanchak was studying at Humberside Collegiate Institute. She describes it as a rival high school to the Etobicoke School of the Arts, where future members of Stars, Metric and Broken Social Scene were enrolled. Kids from the two schools didn't mix, however, and it was years before Yanchak would meet them.

She had started writing songs on an acoustic guitar with her friends, and was listening to a range of alternative music, mostly British bands introduced to her by her older sister. Though she got "really heavy" into The Smiths and Morrissey as a teenager, she also made time for the likes of Moxy Früvous, The Beastie Boys, Tool, Goldie, The Orb and chess club. A serious Björk phase inspired her to experiment with a four-track.

"I didn't know musique actuelle existed but there's a bunch of recordings I have that are very up that alley," she says.

Yanchak also spent her extra-curricular time producing and distributing zines with her friends, and after meeting the founders of Montreal's *Vice* magazine at a zine fair, she joined the ranks of its snarky music critics. It was around this time that she started hanging around Toronto's underground rock scene, populated by a slightly older crowd, including her first proper boyfriend, Simon Nixon. Together, in the summer of 1995, they moved to Montreal.

––––––––

By this time, Britpop had taken hold of the United Kingdom

and attracted a sizeable cult following in Canada. With his Smiths obsession starting to taper off, Lightburn immersed himself in the influx of new records by young guitar bands. He became so enamoured with the scene that he made a pilgrimage to London to stalk Blur guitarist Graham Coxon, Dears demos in hand, at the musicians' hangout du jour, The Good Mixer in Camden.

Anglophilia had a mammoth impact on the band's music, not to mention their increasingly hard drinking habits. Compiled by the band in 2001, *Nor the Dahlias* exposes The Dears' baby steps between 1995 and 1998, when Lightburn's oeuvre was steeped in Blur/Smiths fanaticism.

Crudely recorded and mixed, their first songs, "Everlasting" and "Open Arms", pack in a compelling croon (and a very Morrissey-esque dollop of buffoonish baritone vibrato), jangly guitar work with ultra-'80s exclamations (and one Coxon-esque crunchy solo), open-heart lyrics, buoyant riffs, rubbery basslines and sunny melodies.

The following pair of songs features improved sound, but weaker content. "Nine Eight Two" has the ring of an awkward Blur/Suede fusion, with Lightburn trying on an ill-fitting nasal whine atop slamming guitars and drums. The soft and sincere ballad "The Way the World Treats You" is superior, but still sounds like the ghost of a Morrissey B-side.

The Dears went into their next session to record an EP, *The Future Is Near*. Never released as it was intended, two of its four tracks made it to *Nor the Dahlias*. "Mute Button" could pass for an outtake from Blur's *The Great Escape* were it not for Lightburn's lyrics and vocal delivery on the chorus, which gush flamboyantly with praise and pleas for an object of lovesick affection—even Morrissey has rarely engaged in such vulnerable confessionals. By contrast, "Dear Mr. Pop Star" is cold and clever; warbling '80s synths hover over the intro before a lightly British-accented Lightburn pipes up in his lower register, eerily echoing Damon Albarn. In what was hopefully a wink to a knowing audience, this absolutely shameless bit of Blur pastiche is a song about obsessive fandom, perhaps written on the long ride home from The Good Mixer.

By this point, the band members' virtual alcoholism, personal lives and day jobs began to take a toll on both the progression of the project and their friendships. Though MacDonald had been helpful during at least one recording session, scoring studio time through his brother and helping to finish the mix after Lightburn blacked out, his drunken antics were creating a rift.

"At one point, everyone in the band was forced into a position of punching him out—he was just that kinda guy," Lightburn says. "It's unfortunate. I still love the guy and we had a lot of really amazing times, though most of them revolved around drinking way too much."

After the band had played their first gig in Toronto, White and MacDonald got into a punch-up in the stairwell of the Waverly Hotel, spurred by what Lightburn describes as MacDonald's "retarded" behaviour. White had had enough, and quit the band.

"He was my best friend. It was devastating for him to bail on the project," Lightburn says.

Wounded but far from defeated, The Dears took on a new bassist, Roberto Arquilla, who was a friend of MacDonald's and a fellow Britpop fanatic.

"When we were introduced, Murray said, 'I hear you're a big Smiths fan' and I said, 'Yeah, the biggest,'" recalls Arquilla, "and then Murray said, 'Those are fightin' words!'"

Arquilla had seen The Dears play live and was deeply impressed by their music, so much so that he was intimidated by the prospect of joining the band.

"I really liked the musicianship and the creativity within the parts; they were intricate and so well written. That kind of blew my mind.

"I said, well, 'I'll give it a shot but I'm not as good as Andrew, so if it's not working out, please just can me right away.' I didn't want the music to suffer."

Arquilla proved to be an easy fit in the band, getting along particularly well with Tod. But within weeks of his arrival, the friend who'd gotten him in was out.

"Murray and Richard had been out drinking and they went to get a slice of pizza—it must've been three or four in the morning. Richard was drunk and when he gets drunk, he starts mouthing off and he can really get under people's skin. I got a call from Murray at 4, 4:30 a.m. and he said, 'I just punched Richard in the face and started beating on him.' He felt he'd hit rock bottom."

MacDonald was ejected from the band, relieving some of the tension between the three remaining members, if only briefly. Even Tod, who'd been there from the beginning, had "one foot out" due to the demands of his day job, and Lightburn's apparent downward spiral wasn't encouraging.

"My entire life at this point was falling apart," Lightburn admits. "I was in a relationship for a long time that was falling apart, I was broke, I had no job. Everything was just crumbling, crumbling, crumbling. The Dears were hanging by a thread, but I was determined to not let this one thing die."

Down to one guitarist, the band decided to bring in a keyboardist, briefly taking on The Null Set's Kieran Macnamara, then Mishima's Nick "the Prick" Robinson. The latter was only hired for one gig, but it wasn't long after that show that Lightburn met Yanchak, who was DJing at the St-Laurent blvd. dive Bifteck. He mentioned the encounter to Robinson, who informed Lightburn that she also played keyboards, and recommended her for the band.

"Next thing you know, I was on the phone with Natalia, talking about music," says Lightburn. He invited her to an upcoming Dears show at another St-Laurent dive, Barfly.

"I wasn't really optimistic because I was already jaded at that young age," Yanchak recalls. "I was at CKUT doing the radio show Underground Sounds, which only plays Canadian independent music, so I had a familiarity with the range of stuff that was out there at the time, at least in recorded form.

"But then I really liked them. I actually stayed for the whole show."

"It was a pretty amazing gig," says Lightburn. "We kinda kicked ass. So, soon after that, she said, 'okay, I'm in.'"

During her first two years in Montreal, Yanchak had played keyboards with The Fontonels, featuring Howard Bilerman (who would go on to engineer The Dears' *Orchestral Pop Noir Romantique* five years later), and a bubblegum pop band called The Smile Company, with notable locals Eric Digras, Alex MacSween and Jonathan Cummins. (At The Smile Company's only show, on Valentine's Day 1997, the band shared the stage with The Null Set, with Lightburn sitting in on guitar. It was the first time, as far as Yanchak knows, that they were in the same room together.) Building on basic piano skills, she had already mastered the Farfisa VIP-500 organ, and toyed with a vintage synth called the ARP Axxe, but The Dears took keys a step further.

"The first rehearsals with the band were very challenging," says Yanchak. "I had to learn all these songs that had very specific arrangements, and I had to learn how to use this crazy synth that Murray had, a Korg Polysix."

Even more difficult was the task of raising the band's profile. Between Yanchak's gigs at the McGill University radio station and *Vice* (not to mention the behind-the-scenes work she'd done for her boyfriend's band, The Paper Route), she certainly knew her way around a press kit. At this stage, The Dears had made few attempts at media coverage, let alone a record deal. Lightburn's strategy thus far had been to send a demo to one record company (or hand it to one drunk pop star), and when it was rejected, he'd trash the material and write a new batch of songs, as if some omnipotent jury had judged it and deemed it shit. According to Lightburn, Yanchak was able to identify and remedy the band's business and marketing problems. Without her, he says, they'd still be living hand-to-mouth in a 1 ½ apartment downtown. "No one would have ever heard of The Dears if it weren't for Natalia."

The second incarnation of The Dears recorded what was, again, intended to be a four-song EP, entitled *Chivalry Is Not Dead*. And again, the EP was never released, but two tracks from that session appear on *Nor the Dahlias*. Judging from "Corduroy Boy" and "She's Well Aware", the band's sound had evolved, but their style hadn't. The Blur-ish tendencies remained: the injections of winking humour, the gratuitous la-la-las, the mid-Atlantic accent, the bobbing oompah rhythm, the guitar grind, the chiptune synths and the snakes and ladders bass. But the songwriting, derivative as it was, had tightened up considerably, achieving A-side quality, and with the accompanying strings and horns, and Yanchak's frilly organ backdrop and back-up vocals, a fresh aesthetic was clearly developing.

The introduction of cellist Brigitte Mayes built on the promise of the band's earlier orchestral experiment, "Can't Remember Anything Else". That track had been recorded in early 1996 by a McGill music student (for credit) and featured Lightburn's very first stab at strings. He would he later say they had been "poorly arranged," but the strings actually form an effective, if somewhat simple, backdrop. Still quasi-Britpop in tone, the game-changing song stands out amid the outright mimicry of their other material. There are tender lyrics, earnest lead vocals, a squiggle of silly voices and, hoisted over an introductory piano trill, strings that veer from decorous and dainty to austere and melancholy.

The last song on *Dahlias* is the title track, recorded in 1996 with only an acoustic guitar, a mic, a four-track, a ghetto blaster and headphones. With Lightburn's locomotive strumming, two-part harmonies, classic cascading melody and lyrics that balance the brash ("Sitting here waiting for someone to get in my face"), the romantic ("Nobody else baby, I sing this one only for you") and the clever ("Hey there Dahlia, it isn't over/maybe it's over/baby it's over"), the song, like those from the *Chivalry* EP, points the way forward.

CHAPTER 2
This could just be love

"To this day, no one's doing that kind of music.
No one out there sounds like The Dears."

Though things were looking up for The Dears in some respects, relationships within the band and on the periphery were still in disarray, as was Lightburn. With pain in the heart and keyboard and string arrangements on the brain, his state was practically bipolar. In his more manic phases, he wrote an album's worth of material; under the influence of depression, he'd indulge in booze and drugs.

One manifestation of his creative mania during this period was an obsessive-compulsive need to document the influx of sounds and song ideas in his head and in his midst.

"I just lived behind Natalia's four-track," he says. "I would carry it around everywhere in a little briefcase, and I had a little microphone and a little cable so I could record something as it came in. That was really important to me at the time. If anyone thinks I'm self-absorbed now, wow, it pales in comparison to where I was at then. But, in a way, that's the beauty and the romance of it."

Somehow, Lightburn, Yanchak, Arquilla, Tod, Mayes and a number of guests managed to record an album, and in the ritzy Montreal neighbourhood of Westmount, no less. They set up a makeshift studio in the family home of Andy Vial, the drummer from The Null Set, who were also recording an album there.

"His parents were out of town for a few months, and we basically turned the place upside down, no respect, no regard," says Yanchak—Arquilla concurs, saying they "drank the house dry and passed out while recording."

"Murray basically didn't sleep," Yanchak says, "'cause he would engineer The Null Set sessions during the day and then The Dears would record our stuff during the night."

Lightburn remembers an overnight mixing session in a bedroom where two Null Set band members were sleeping, the night before all of his band's rented gear had to be returned.

"I sat in a chair at the desk, mixing on headphones till the sun came up. I didn't get out of the chair for eight hours, not even to go to the bathroom. Andy and Missy were asleep three feet away, and when I was finished, they were just waking up."

Given the band's limited resources, they certainly couldn't get the brass section they wanted, not to mention other, more fundamental things. "We had to record it on one reel 'cause we couldn't afford two, so we had to play the reel slower," Arquilla says. "But it was fun—it felt homey, in a way."

Despite his fond memories, Arquilla also recalls the day, in 1999, not long after recording had wrapped, when he had to tell Lightburn that he and Tod were quitting the band.

"I was kind of insufferable, and I could see people that I had known for a long time pulling away from me," Lightburn says, "and Rob was one of them, because he didn't like what I was becoming."

Arquilla agrees, but also remembers feeling at odds with what the band was becoming, as though there'd been an evolution in style that had passed him by.

"I really liked what the band was when it was Andrew, John and Murray, and I wanted to keep going in that vein. The songs that were coming out were still well written, but very different, with more layers. It was starting to get complicated when I wanted to just bash out really cool pop tunes."

"We were at Bifteck and I remember Murray being totally dishevelled, telling me how shitty things were, and then I basically had to drop it on him that we were leaving the band. He was pretty destroyed by that."

"It was a crazy transitional time," Lightburn says. "We'd made this album together and it was amazing but there was a lot of stuff going on around it that was pulling us away from each other.

"So, for the first time, [Natalia and I] had a full, mastered record that we were really proud of, and no one to play it."

———

Like a fresh Gallic breeze from the other side of the Channel, the sound of France weighs heavily on The Dears' debut album, *End of a Hollywood Bedtime Story*, offsetting the wanton anglophilia of the past. This came in the wake of pop culture phenomena from overseas and down the street: Stereolab, a British (and largely English-language) band with a French-accented singer, whose blend of Moog synths and guitars had been "busting the lid off the shit," according to Yanchak, throughout the '90s; Air's 1998 debut album, *Moon Safari*, with its gauzy strings and horns, clunky keyboards and space-age lounge sounds; the syrupy symphonies of accordionist and composer Francis Lai, as heard by Lightburn, Yanchak recalls, on the soundtrack of the *Emmanuelle* films (softcore porn that screened on local TV station TQS's weekly program, *Bleu Nuit*); and the C'est Extra DJ nights at Montreal's Cabaret Music Hall, where doses of vintage French pop were administered monthly. Among the most popular tunes at C'est Extra were the orchestral pop creations of Serge Gainsbourg.

When it was released in 2000, many critics compared *Hollywood*'s aesthetic to that of Pulp, who Lightburn claimed to have rarely listened to. Besides a shared emphasis on keyboards and synths, the two bands drew from the same sources, though they didn't always grasp at the same elements. On songs such as "His 'N' Hers" and "This Is Hardcore", Pulp's Jarvis Cocker echoed Gainsbourg's penchant for perverse narratives, partly spoken in a hushed baritone, with the odd orgasmic exclamation. The latter song's use of strings evokes Gainsbourg all the more, but strings were an anomaly for Pulp.

The Dears have never indulged in overtly sexual lyrical themes the way Gainsbourg did, but they did embrace his approach to chamber rock arrangements and crescendo-and-climax song structures. His landmark 1971 album *Histoire de Melody Nelson* features the same kind of orchestral ebb and flow, and interplay between cello, violins and electric and acoustic guitars, heard on songs such as "Where the World Begins and Ends", *Bedtime Story*'s instrumental centrepiece. Prominent strings and synths came to define The Dears' aesthetic, and even though their debut album's melodies bob, catch and soar, and grinding rock riffs are occasionally front and centre, the band's instrumentation set them comfortably apart from Britpop, a wave that rolled back by the turn of the millennium.

————

Much like Britpop's backwash, by 2000, the North American indie rock scene had become increasingly twee, infused with folk, country and pale pop influences that mollified guitars and calmed paces. By contrast, *Hollywood* bursts open with "C'était pour la passion", vocals at the forefront, followed by a bubbly bassline, chiming keys and shimmering synths. Rock rears its head with a dual guitar and keyboard cacophony on "Jazz Waltz No. 3 in B Flat", thinning out in the verses with keys that mimic a harpsichord before the wall of noise is re-erected. The song is also notable for its telling Lightburn/Yanchak harmony, repeated climactic cries of "LOVE!"

The record's first single was "This Is a Broadcast", a relay from wiry guitar to cello and violins to piano and organ to drums and percussion to vocals that are very much in the key of Morrissey. There's a roughness to the assembly of this song, one that extends to the record as a whole that actually makes these complementary parts pop more than they should. Each element is distinct, and despite a clumsy middle-eight where all instruments and supporting vocals carry the melody simultaneously, this unevenness lends extra tension to a skilfully played, well-orchestrated track.

For those who like it really rough, "Heartless Romantic", another of the album's singles, is a song rubbed raw. The mourning of a dying relationship is rendered with gritty, distorted lead vocal and drum tracks, paired with relatively clean organ and piano. Particularly striking, is the volley between lead and backing vocals, the latter more like a chorus re-interpreting the lead's expressions of agony, a harmony contrasting Lightburn's lowest register with Yanchak's highest.

For a song about despair and self-destruction, its lilt and pacing is upbeat in the tradition of bands like The Smiths. The melodies are so pretty and buoyant, you can almost see the bouncing ball rebounding off lyrics like, "Don't have any money (pockets are empty), don't have any looks (he is a dog), just borrowed pianos (I'm coming over) that I can hardly play (to use what I want to)." The lyrics are woeful, and tinges of melancholy are embedded in the piano, keys and vocal melody. But it's Lightburn's deliriously impassioned delivery, with distortion pushing it even closer to the brink of disintegration, that packs the emotive sucker punch into what is otherwise a cleverly constructed piece of heartbroken pop.

Another such song is the title track, an even livelier, polished pop tune than the last. Like "C'était pour la passion", the song gets off to a gallop straight out of the gate, drums and vocals simultaneously establishing a brisk beat and setting the tone for a story that's "so very sad." It's a classic confused parting letter from a lover scorned to the woman who's leaving him, featuring blame, bitterness, self-pity and a bold promise to turn a new leaf without her, with a postscript subtly pleading for reconciliation, just in case she's still wavering. There are more references to self-sabotage and self-destructive behaviour as our hero bemoans his addiction to the kind of hand-wringing, dropping-to-your-knees drama that seems to fuel this five-minute opera.

Though the rhythm is tapered down for the chorus, where keys and synths form an ethereal foundation for Lightburn's soaring vocals, the adrenaline doesn't abate until the song's very last seconds. The now familiar guitar crank adds backbone to hyperactive drums then reverberates loudly through the song's transition from verse to chorus. And, matching the sense of grudging acceptance that this love story is concluding as it should, with its hero in ruins, the song ends adrift, leaving only lightly warped strains of piano and organ in the wake of electric riffage, pounding drums and vocals that, by song's end, had overshot Earth's atmosphere.

Following these two explosive death rattles for romance, the epic "There Is No Such Thing as Love" announces itself as an elegy, with crowd noise and a funereal melody on the organ. It's an admittedly cynical, resoundingly histrionic expression of dejection and depression. Among the dramatic heights hit throughout the track's 10 minutes is Lightburn's cry of "LET ME GIVE IT TO YOU STRAY-AIGHT!" (this is undoubtedly where the gospel choir would've chimed in if the band's budget had allowed it), as well as the titular mantra, sung by Yanchak, that kicks in near the song's midway point, backed by more high-flying cries from Lightburn. After a false ending, guitars duel and a guitar and keyboard duet, climaxing in a series of spectral guitar moans.

The album closes with "Partir, Par Terre", a brief but hopeful coda that evokes amusement park carousels and waltzers with its dizzy organ and bobbing piano, strings and drums. There are echoes of earlier Dears material here, via Blur's whimsical Old Britannia, like a glance over the shoulder at a past that the band just left in the dust.

––––––––––

"For the first time, I was really going to do something with this. I was determined and I wasn't letting anything stand in my way."

Scraping himself off the floor, where a romantic breakup and the near disintegration of his band had left him, Lightburn scaled back on the self-destructive behaviour and set out to finally release a record. Joining forces with Yanchak made this possible, and not only because of her industry savvy. With band membership down to three (and Mayes was only involved part-time), it was already becoming evident to Lightburn that he and Yanchak were the nucleus of the project. He now considers this revelation—along with his simultaneous self-rehabilitation, career motivation and musical evolution—to have constituted an epiphany. Not that that made his life easy.

"An epiphany is kind of like a car wreck; the next thing you know, your car's upside down and there's smoke coming out of the engine and you're bleeding, but somehow you got from before that to after that, and you're changed."

Of course, the chemistry between Lightburn and Yanchak wasn't entirely musical. When they met, they were both on the outs with their significant others, and their respective journeys to splitsville were expedited by budding feelings for each other.

"There was obviously a romantic element to my relationship with Natalia that kind of started, stopped, started, stopped," he says. "Meanwhile we were in a band together so we'd argue about the band and then we'd argue about the relationship and what it was, 'cause there was no definition to it."

This soap opera played out on the sidelines as the duo was auditioning new members and sending demos to record companies. The remnants of the *Hollywood* crew were soon joined by guitarist Jonathan Cohen, bassist Martin Pelland and drummer George Donoso III.

"They were walking into a house that was already built, and essentially they were given the job of helping to decorate that house," says Lightburn, explaining his M.O. for integrating new blood into the band.

"I didn't want to be a dictator and say, 'Play it like this.' I wanted people to put some personality into it once they were familiar with the music. That's part of the unwritten policy of The Dears."

As much as each member contributed to the band's sound, it's Lightburn's personality and frenzied mind that would determine the way the new songs were played live. When they finally signed a contract with the fledgling Montreal label Grenadine Records, self-described specialists in "timeless pop attitude," he had a wild idea for a live show.

"I was really drunk, and I was telling [Natalia] about how I wanted to get brass and strings, all this music that I hear in my head, and try to make it happen live. She just told me I was crazy, 'you can't do it.' A lot of people were telling me that. I remember [fellow local musician] Jon Ascensio telling me, 'What do you want, man? It's just indie rock.'"

In those days, an indie rock band larger than a quintet was an uncommon sight, and on the rare occasion that you'd see horns and strings, it was usually a gimmick, practically a prop. But Lightburn convinced Yanchak that going orchestral was a worthwhile experiment, and they went about finding players.

One of the violinists they tried to bring on board was Jessica Moss, who had co-founded the art rock band A Silver Mt. Zion (part of the godspeed you! black emperor family) that year. "I just knew that she played violin, I had no idea that she was so far out of my league," Lightburn says. "We were showing her these fucking horrible charts that I had printed out on this shitty program 'cause I didn't even know how to read music. I had no idea what I was doing, nor did I even pretend to. She practically laughed my sorry ass out of her apartment."

Nevertheless, a brass and strings octet dubbed the Cosmopolitan City Orchestra—most of them McGill-trained with one foot in the Montreal Symphony Orchestra, according to Lightburn—made their debut with The Dears in 1999, all 14 of them squeezing onto the small stage at Petit Campus. Roughly six months later, when *Hollywood* dropped in June 2000, the band presented a second orchestral blowout, with Lightburn alternating between impassioned singing, guitar-slinging and manically conducting the CCO.

"The best memory of that was when Howard Bilerman told me that it was like watching a train without brakes," Lightburn recalls, laughing heartily at what he describes as "making a fool out of myself in front of 400 people."

"We were so under-rehearsed, it was a joke. I imagine that it was the worst show in Dears history."

To the untrained indie rock ear, however, the show was stunning, and in that period, in this country, utterly unique. Following a significant push from local media, whose critics highly praised *Hollywood* and the band's live show, The Dears began to pop up in print and on the airwaves across the country, particularly in Toronto, where *Eye Weekly* called them "officially the best band in Canada." Their series of increasingly well attended shows there culminated with a coup during Canadian Music Week, in March 2001.

"We sold out the Horseshoe Tavern, which was fucking insane. I remember we finished the soundcheck and we were leaving the club, going to get sushi or whatever, and there was a line-up around the fucking block, with people getting turned away. That blew my mind. When I made *Hollywood*, I never saw that shit coming down the pike. For a little indie band that was on a label that was being run out of some dude's apartment, it was pretty cool."

CHAPTER 3

You've got my soul, I've got your heart

"For our next album, we're building this monument that will perhaps be the last record for The Dears. Because of all the work that Natalia and I do managing the band and the amount of effort we put into our live show...what's that saying? 'The star that burns brightest...' [laughs]. You know what I mean: live fast, die young."

HAVING CONQUERED TORONTO, the band hoped to open a new front in the United States. To date, their only stateside appearance was a showcase at the '00 edition of the NYC industry festival CMJ, where they'd shared a bill with Stars, a like-minded band formed in Toronto that had recently moved en masse to Montreal. The Dears spent a good chunk of the day trying to track down a stray box of *Hollywood* CDs that Grenadine had sent over—in those early days of the internet, CDs were essential, serving as business cards as well as merch. But even if the band had wanted to connect with U.S. labels, their contract with Grenadine forbade it; the bedroom operation had exclusive rights to distribute the record in North America.

"Looking back, they were just doing their job," says Yanchak, "but we grew to a point where we needed more from our label than they had the means to give."

Unable to properly promote and release *Hollywood* in the States, or offer tour support or an advance for the next record, Grenadine was nevertheless owed another album. Having signed the contract without consulting a lawyer, the band hired a "ball breaker" of a legal representative, who strongly encouraged them to get out of the deal. The compromise was giving Grenadine *Nor the Dahlias*, the compilation of old Dears material served up with some acerbic liner notes care of Lightburn, complete with quotes from The Smiths' "Paint a Vulgar Picture", a song about a record company's plan to profit from the death of a musician on their roster, "only we're still alive." Lightburn also wrote: "I have less than a week to hand these recordings to Grenadine or the Contract Police may come after us for months...I actually find it really sad how this record is finding its way into your precious hands."

"I feel in some ways a little badly about it because I don't think they deserved that," says Yanchak, "but at the same time, they should've just let us do our thing."

After being asked to contribute a track to a compilation on a newly minted Toronto label, Shipbuilding, the band made a counter-offer, proposing that Shipbuilding release their next record, an EP. The label promptly dropped the compilation idea, making The Dears' EP its very first release.

Over four distinctly different songs, the band pushed their stylistic boundaries, exhibiting rock bombast, sultry balladry, parlour funk and acoustic dirge. Working with Bilerman at Hotel2Tango, the producer/studio combo behind myriad Montreal-made records, the band was on firmer sonic ground than ever. With the EP's title, they riffed on the buzz words favoured by their critics: *Orchestral Pop Noir Romantique*.

It opens wide with "Heathrow or Deathrow", its melody gracefully ascending and descending, like a tap dance up and down a staircase, with a cascading guitar riff and tumbling rhythm during the verses, and strings and keys sashaying during the transition; then, in the largely instrumental chorus, charging arm in arm with guitars and heftier synths, like a bulbous, sonic barrage. Despite its familiar theme of troubled romance, the lyrics bear a heightened sense of desperation, nearly matching the musical drama; though reconciliation may be in the making, the protagonist is determined to cross an ocean for resolution with his lover, and the repeated line "there's only one way" implies that plan B could call for drastic action.

"Autonomy" continues to cast romance against an epic backdrop, this time striking a tone that's thematically apocalyptic and musically lux and decadent. Lightburn tones down the emotional turmoil and focuses instead on the intensity of a relationship that's working in an environment that's not: "And while the world falls apart/you've got my soul, I've got your heart." Evoking Gainsbourg again, the track starts off sparse, just a haunting synth trill and drums, joined by single notes on a keyboard. Guitars only appear after the first verse, with another minimal, picked melody. Cello glides into play in the second verse, at once refined and raunchy, as does a touch of vocal from Yanchak, harmonizing with Lightburn about "delayed metros" and "drug or Cheminaud." Sounding more girlish than usual, Yanchak compounds the Gainsbourgian tone by echoing his wife and collaborator, Jane Birkin. The song edges into another orbit with a brief, disjointed guitar solo before Lightburn delivers the last verse with greater volume and a touch of falsetto, then wraps the track with ethereal "ahhhh-ahs" in harmony with Yanchak.

On "No Return", a strange choice for a single, The Dears veer into soft-focus '70s vibes, contrasting wan piano plonks and guitar strums with a prominent flute, funky guitar gurgles and a near-baggy beat. The song's see-saw vocal melody verges on awkward, while the couplet "Cash flow, [in a French accent] *radio*, let me GO-OH-OH-OH, OH-OH-OH, OH-OH-OH" is flamboyant to the point of being funny. From there, the track drags for over a minute before climaxing in style with some sweet drum fills and a flurry of flute.

Bringing the EP down even further—in mood, not quality—is "Acoustic Guitar Phase", in which Lightburn seems to despair about his and the band's future. Singing in a hushed, artificially high register, he keeps it remarkably close to deadpan. It's The Dears' catatonic take on "I Know It's Over", but where Morrissey sang "Oh Mother, I can feel the soil falling over my head," Lightburn, assuming a naysayer's voice, sings "Nigger, you're crazy, go back to your dad and mom." Backed only by hard strumming for the first four minutes, his vocals fade to a chant in the last two, making way for some subdued, almost submerged flute and horns, ending the *OPNR* EP[12] on a dark but graceful note.

———————

Released seven weeks prior to September 11th, 2001, *OPNR*'s desperate and doomy lyrics seemed eerily timely. Once retaliation for the attacks was underway and Canada joined the U.S. in the war in Afghanistan, the collective shock and grief over the events of that day wore off, and scepticism returned. Like most people, I understood the motivation behind Afghanistan. But when it became clear, very early in the game, that the "War on Terror" would likely extend to Iraq, Iran or North Korea (or the entire "axis of evil"), people like myself, who'd never paid much attention to American foreign policy, began to take notice. In January of 2003, when the Iraq war was increasingly imminent, vast numbers

———————

12 It's difficult for me to separate these songs, particularly "Heathrow or Deathrow", from the circumstances under which I listened to them in the fall of 2001. I heard about the collapse of the World Trade Center roughly 90 minutes after the second tower fell. After making a few phone calls from my part-time job (including one to Lightburn, who held the phone up to his TV so I could hear the live feed from CNN), I snuck out mid-shift and walked through downtown Montreal to the office of the *Mirror*, where I'm still employed as a music journalist and copy editor—at the time, some of the people closest to me worked there, too. During the 25-minute trek, I couldn't help keeping my eyes on the perfectly blue sky, nearly colliding with other people doing the same; occasionally I'd pass panicked crowds evacuated from buildings in our financial sector—we also have a World Trade Centre (the Centre commercial du monde) just blocks away from the *Mirror*. The music emanating from my headphones during that walk was *OPNR*, with its talk of planes, "prey on us, desperation's advantageous," "looks like it's gonna come down soon," "as our world falls apart."

of Canadians took to the streets to let Prime Minister Jean Chrétien know that they didn't want their country mixed up in what appeared to be a venture motivated by greed. In Montreal, where anti-war sentiment is especially high due to the anti-imperialist Québécois factor, nearly half a million people flooded the downtown streets one Saturday afternoon in near-Arctic temperatures. I, who'd never been to a demo in my life, was one of them. And I had a new Dears EP to listen to.

The *Protest* EP was made during a strange time for The Dears. Two weeks prior to recording their sophomore album in the spring of 2002, guitarist Jonathan Cohen had quit the band.

"I loved the band, and shared a lot of great musical moments with them which are unforgettable, powerful," he says. "But I felt more and more alienated from my own musical ambitions, and The Dears were starting to take up a lot of my energy. In the end, I had nothing left in me to give to the band."

Unable to fill the vacancy in time, Lightburn played all the album's guitar parts himself.

"My fingers, after five days of playing 10 hours a day, were destroyed," he recalls. "I actually had to stop playing because my hands were cut and swollen. It was disgusting."

There was plenty of time for healing, however, given their producer Brenndan McGuire's main gig as sound engineer for Sloan, who were frequently on tour. Even after the on-again off-again tracking process wrapped, McGuire's mix was a long time coming.

While they were waiting, they hired a new guitarist, Rob

Benvie, formerly of the beloved Halifax band Thrush Hermit. They had met him during the *Hollywood* tour, when he was playing with Mike O'Neill (onetime leader of Haligonian via Kingston act, The Inbreds), and they were the sweat act.

"I heard their name and saw George [Donoso] and Jon Cohen wearing leather jackets and I kinda assumed that they were gonna be some shitty garage band, so I wasn't really that interested in hearing them," says Benvie. "But they were awesome that night. And I did something I rarely do, which is buy a record from the band after the show."

Within a year, Benvie moved to Montreal to study English at Concordia University. With next to no friends in town, he accepted an invite to a house party from Donoso, whom he'd run into on the street the very day that he moved. He struck up an acquaintance with a few of the band members and became a fixture at some of the bars and restaurants on St-Laurent.

"We were all sitting in La Cabane talking about where the fuck we were gonna get a guitar player. Martin [Pelland] had recommended Benvie on the strength of his solo stuff and a few minutes later, the guy literally walked right past us. We knocked on the window and called him over. He sat down with us and I asked him, 'Are you a good guitar player?' and Benvie said, 'I'm the best.' And that was it."

"It was funny," Benvie says, "'cause I'd been feeling pretty lonely, thinking that I'd been in bands my whole life up until then, and maybe I was done playing indie rock."

He was hardly done. But Brigitte Mayes, after recording her cello, keyboard and flute parts for the second album, "slipped out the back door" to pursue a teaching career.

Though they were sorry to see her go, and felt slightly betrayed by another loss so soon after Cohen's departure, the cello had proven to be an impractical part of the band's show, and one they've never reintegrated.

"Towards the end, when she was still in the band, we basically stopped using the cello live because it never came out right," Lightburn says. "It's a piece of fucking wood and a bow. If I can make the part audible through a sampler and a keyboard, I'll do that, because I'd rather have the sound than the decoration."

The band, Benvie included, immersed themselves in recording *Protest*. "It was an oasis; it renewed our hope and optimism when people were quitting and things were getting really dark," Yanchak says. Scott Harding, who's engineered the likes of The Crash Test Dummies, Medeski, Martin & Wood and The Wu-Tang Clan, mixed the EP in his Brooklyn apartment. Lightburn was fascinated by his methods, calling him "a true artist, a genius."

"His approach was all about love, it was from the guts," Lightburn says. "He stands up and waves his hands around and he wants to make sure the speakers are moving, which is brilliant. I like extreme mixes. Most of the music on the radio is mixed by the same two or three hosers, and it's all gross. Nobody's taking chances anymore. I remember listening to that first mix on headphones and getting shivers all over my body. And [Harding] had said the most hilarious thing, he said, 'You hear that vocal, man? That's John Lennon beaming in from outer space, dude!'"

———

Released five months before the Iraq war began in March

of 2003, and just days after the Bali nightclub bombing, the *Protest* EP seemed to embody the volatility of the times. Lightburn's new revolutionary look, featuring a military helmet and megaphone, cemented the project's dissenting spirit. Although *Protest* was recorded during the aftermath of 9/11, it had been conceived around the time of the infamous Summit of the Americas protests in Quebec City, in April of 2001, when demonstrations were primarily anti-globalization affairs. And The Dears were not impressed.

"One of the things that inspired the lyrics was being constantly asked to play benefit shows," says Yanchak. "This one time, we asked what the benefit was for, and it was like, 'Oh, it's so me and my friends can rent a bus and go down to protest at the G-whatever, G8 thing in Ottawa,' and we were just like, What? That is idiotic. A bunch of upper middle class kids who can afford to go to university and they want us to play a benefit concert so they can rent a party bus? It was so offensive. I'm sure they had some good intentions, but is that the best way, considering how much work it is for us? People take that shit for granted.

"That was a defining moment for us," she adds, "realizing that this is our career, this is our path that we've chosen and some people are viewing it as just this fun thing you do on the side, between classes."

Yanchak isn't anti-activist, however, acknowledging the validity of resistance, civil disobedience and even revolution when circumstances call for it. She also concedes that the band had a change of heart vis à vis the demo scene, which, by late 2002, had grown, broadened and shifted its focus to protesting war.

"It's your right as a human being to be a shit-disturber when you don't like what's going on, and I think that's what the *Protest* EP embodies," she says. "Because it happened so concurrently with the events of 9/11, it resonated a lot for the band."

As Lightburn said at the time, "It was really important for us to say something about what's happening to our world."

Presented as one piece in three distinct movements, *Protest* peaks early with "Heaven Have Mercy on Us", its titular choral refrain booming operatically like the cry of a besieged people, backed by a surging sonic frenzy. Out of the first movement's ashes rises the cool, deceptively detached "Summer of Protest", with its single note piano, Talking Heads' "Psycho Killer" bassline and deadpan vocals, which eventually escalate to a triple threat of megaphone shouts, stinging guitars and a siren. The coda, a devastating piano ballad called "No Hope Before Destruction", comes closer to familiar Dears terrain, with its bleak beauty and apocalyptic setting.

In keeping with the spirit of the record, the packaging for the first 500 copies were painstakingly produced by the band between Arquilla's parents' garage in Rosemère, QC, (a Montreal suburb) and Yanchak's father's testing lab workshop in Mississauga, ON. The other DIY touch, which was much less common in 2002 than it is now, especially for a somewhat established band, was releasing the EP independently. Without a record deal or a sophomore album in the can, the band was in limbo, and *Protest* provided purpose.

"It gave us a sense of accomplishment," says Lightburn, "and a reason to go out on the road and discuss our plan of action."

CHAPTER 4
Let's just keep fighting the end of the world

"Sure, there's no security in this band, but there's no security anywhere in life. That's why the record is called *No Cities Left*, because there's no escape, nowhere is safe, nobody really has a home."

IN THE WAKE OF *Orchestral Pop Noir Romantique*, when The Dears were Canada's biggest unsigned band, major labels started circling overhead. After entering into a courtship with one label, despite all the wining and dining, Lightburn felt that the process "ate away at The Dears like a cancer."

"It was pretty brutal," Yanchak confirms. "We were just trying to do our thing and then we've got these guys dangling unknown fortunes in front of us, trying to impress us. One night we were out drinking with one of the A&R guys and he said, 'Murray, just write a goddamn hit. Write a goddamn hit,' and that fucked [Murray] up. What do you do? How do you react? And writing a song, pouring it out and performing it is such a creative and intimate means of communicating your deepest thoughts and emotions. For Murray as a songwriter, it really threw him for a loop."

In the end, The Dears joined MapleMusic (distributed by Universal), a new label that Lightburn's longtime friend Sam Roberts had recently signed to, one that didn't demand hits or an epic commitment.

"There's always the threat that The Dears will be over tomorrow—that's part of what makes it so exciting for us," Lightburn said in 2003. "But that's why it was hard to lock down a record deal, 'cause they always wanna sign you for 10 albums. We're constantly on the verge of collapse, so we can't see that far ahead. I mean, there might not even be a world two albums from now," he said, reflecting on the pervasive paranoia of the time, just before the U.S. invasion of Iraq. Yanchak added, "At least then we'd be released from the contract." With the world raging outside, the band's inner sanctum felt unstable and strained by line-up shifts and a workload where administration ("rock 'n' roll business," as Lightburn called it) was outweighing creativity. And then McGuire delivered his mix of their sophomore album.

It had been his and the band's first digital production— and a mammoth one at that, with heaps of keyboard, guitar, string, horn, woodwind, vocal, percussion and drum tracks— and rather than deleting bad takes as they were recorded, thereby isolating the good takes of each part, he had kept everything, creating a mountain of data that was, in the end, impossible to scale. With all the intermittent Sloan tours, and his impending commitment to record Sam Roberts' debut album, McGuire was unable to devote enough time to the project. According to Yanchak, the express mix was riddled with bad takes, shoddy editing and dirty tracks that featured, for example, Mayes' inhalations before she put her mouth to the flute.

"Brenndan was fantastic to work with, but the project took on a life that was so huge, it turned into *Apocalypse Now,*" Lightburn says. "The night we listened to that first mix, I sat there with my head in my hands thinking song after song, 'Can't put this out, can't put this out, can't put this out.'"

"I just sat there with the rest of the band thinking, 'A year later, where's our fucking album?'" Yanchak says. "So we lost our shit, which we do very well. And, again, we almost broke up."

And so they turned to Bilerman, who freed up the fully booked Hotel2Tango to let Lightburn do damage control. The studio is, to this day, co-run by Efrim Menuck of godspeed you! black emperor, and whether this was a help or a hindrance, Menuck's dead dog literally infiltrated the atmosphere (and possibly the gear) during one of Lightburn's marathon shifts.

"When we broke Efrim's urn, with his dog's ashes inside, I really thought somebody had put a curse on us," says Lightburn. "I don't know Efrim, but I was expecting the worst. Luckily he was cool. He understood that we were flailing, just trying desperately to mix our record. Basically, it felt like delivering 12 babies. It was retarded."

On the eighth day, Lightburn rested. Or maybe just got hammered. But somehow, the band, despite the duress, the limited funds and the divided loyalties, managed to meet their grandiose ambitions and manoeuvre all that raw data into something spectacular. They credit their guest players, including Sam Roberts—a closet virtuoso violinist—and the Brébeuf Brass (featuring Chris Seligman and Evan Cranley of Stars), with helping to achieve a near-symphonic sound.

"The only reason we were able to make this record a little closer to what we envisioned [than *Hollywood*] is because we have a lot of brilliant friends who play music," Lightburn said shortly after the album was released. "I wasn't placing ads or calling people in the guild book, I wanted to keep it close, so we just had a few people playing a bunch of tracks, and they played so beautifully. There's just more love that way."

———

One of the driving ideas behind *No Cities Left*, the album that would eventually come out of this mess, was "a big love, a love that can bring us together and save the world." Though its narratives may wallow in negativity and its characters may thrive on melancholia, the album's grandeur, urgency and anthemic propulsion effectively convey that "big love" is at once a weapon and the thing that makes the fight worthwhile.

The album lifts off with such force that the rest is practically a comedown. The epic "We Can Have It" gracefully glides into play with soft vocals and a slow, gentle melody, rendered via barely there acoustic guitar and keys. Offsetting a lullaby quality are lyrics about dreams invaded by "all the horrible things in life," and a quixotic search for "what we want." Suddenly the drums kick in, dropping an insistent beat buoyed by a sonorous guitar line, around which a second guitar and melodica weave while strings undulate and maracas shake. The crashing climax comes as the whole fleet, brass included, charges forward, with Lightburn shouting the refrain "You're not alone!" Then the barrage scales back, the drums disappear, the trumpet fades, leaving only ghostly synths and the final refrain: "It won't ever be what we want." In the final seconds, Lightburn's voice disappears into a chilling group chant.

Before the goosebumps have receded, "Who Are You, Defenders of the Universe?" announces itself with a stark guitar chime and drum pattern reminiscent of David Bowie's "Five Years" (on which drummer Woody Woodmansey reportedly tried to put "hopelessness into a drumbeat"). The song is a Kafka-esque parable that could just as easily be based on record company bullshit or the American war machine.

The album's lead single was "Lost in the Plot", with its dense wall of synths, downcast guitars and pretty vocal melody sung in Lightburn's most effeminate croon, one of his many voices. Many fans will cry sacrilege, but this song has always bored me, despite its sonic and melodic debt to The Smiths and Suede, who were once my favourite bands. Sat beside the eclectic, imposing aesthetics that make *No Cities Left* so fresh, "Lost in the Plot" seems stale. While the record's other Britpop throwback, "Don't Lose the Faith", sounds like a companion piece to The Smiths' "There Is a Light That Never Goes Out", its melody and lyrics make it far superior to "Lost in the Plot", at least to my ears.

"Expect the Worst/Cos She's a Tourist" commands attention with an arch intro, fitted with an odd time signature, amusingly disjointed lyrics, aggressive violins and bombastic, operatic backing vocals. Then the pace slows to a crawl, the symphonic cacophony replaced by lush keys and brass, and the lyrics, doled out piecemeal over six minutes, evoking the suicidal tendencies of a decadent narcissist.

Noisy fanfare marks the start of Side Two, and the Gainsbourgian drama of "Pinned Together Falling Apart". From understated beginnings, the song builds to a screaming finale, with actual screaming, squealing guitars and another heavy, quasi-choral backing vocal. "Never Destroy Us" is another album highlight, kicking in with luscious violins and a rise and fall vocal melody, care of Lightburn and Yanchak in harmony, that accentuates mild funk and femininity. As if morphing from a dancer to a drill sergeant, the song ends with a stunner, a slamming beat and distorted shouting.

"22: The Death of All the Romance" is The Dears' first real duet. Lightburn and Yanchak's bickering exchange, and the guitars that propel it, recall "Ciao!", the break-up duet by Lush's Miki Berenyi and Pulp's Jarvis Cocker. But "22" is more complex, sophisticated and theatrical, particularly the passage where Lightburn seems to channel Edith Piaf. Sadly, the mix does not serve Yanchak well, leaving her voice flat and dull.

"Postcard From Purgatory" is a mostly instrumental, eight-minute epic built piece by piece: faraway guitar distortion, a slow drum beat, a tambourine, sultry melodica, cello and acoustic guitar roll out over the first two-and-a-half minutes, like Bowie's version of The Beach Boys' "Wild Is the Wind", infiltrated by an obnoxious waft of Gauloises smoke. Deadpan gang vocals appear next, then a few words from Lightburn ("empty heads/mouths/hearts/souls"), and finally some galloping drum fills and crackling synths, brass and strings, all of it draped in reverb, emanating sleaze. The song emerges from a false ending with a searing combination of a flute vamp and drilling riffage, ending à la Zeppelin with a slow guitar stomp and gargantuan drums.

Though almost any song seems like a coda in the wake of "Purgatory", the title track wraps the record with high drama. It begins like a French pop nugget, with a plodding beat, arpeggiated acoustic guitar, tangoing melodicas and girlish backup vocals again echoing Jane Birkin. With the appearance of electric guitar, the song slowly grows into a chamber rock throwdown, ending in a flurry of brash drums and shrill violins, seemingly ripped from one of Bernard Herman's Hitchcock soundtracks.

Rendering such a surging, sweeping record live required an extra pair of hands, and Valérie Jodoin-Keaton was eager to assist. As the girlfriend of bassist Martin Pelland, and an amateur rock 'n' roll photographer, she was already a fixture in Dears-world, and after Mayes's departure, she "muscled her way in," as Lightburn put it back in 2003.

"She was pretty amazing because when she joined the band, she was not a musician," Yanchak says. "She was like a sponge, a jack of all trades. She learned to play the flute, she learned all of Brigitte's [keyboard and flute] parts. And she could sing in a higher register—my voice is in a lower register—so it worked out well."

With their "estrogen balance" back to normal, The Dears tested their new line-up, along with Lightburn's megaphone and military head gear, on a short regional jaunt that they called the *Protest* tour. They packed houses in major cities, and occasionally bombed in between—Benvie remembers

Lightburn busting a chair in frustration after playing to a nearly empty room in Sudbury. But the response in some of the smaller towns surprised them.

"We were on that Southern Ontario university circuit that I had done to death with Thrush Hermit, so I wasn't really that excited about it," Benvie says. "But it was really funny that The Dears, which I thought of as being an arty, slightly off-the-wall band, somehow really appealed to the frat hoser guys—I guess maybe it's the wailing guitars or whatever. I remember doing a show in Waterloo and we're setting up and these two total jock guys are right in front of the stage, ready to rock out, and one guy says to the other, 'We got our beers, we got our Dears, what more can we ask for?'"

Backed by college radio play and a little rotation for "Lost in the Plot" on Toronto radio station The Edge, the band continued to build a Canadian audience, hesitantly accepting an invitation to support mainstream Canadian singer songwriter Matthew Good on a lengthy, dues paying nationwide tour. It began on March 20, 2003 three weeks prior to the mid-April release of *No Cities Left*, and on the same day that the U.S. invaded Iraq with "shock and awe."

"The Matthew Good tour was really big and his crowd kinda ate up our schtick," says Benvie, "but he was insufferable. I have no problem going on the record and saying that Matt Good is a fucking clown. He was very confident in his own political beliefs so he'd do these speeches every night. He was acting like he was at the epicentre of something that was really meaningful and big, but we were just like, 'Ugh, let's just get this tour over with.' He really wanted to be buddies, with Murray especially. It was pretty gross."

Good was just one of many Canadian artists trying to siphon some street cred from The Dears. David Usher (onetime frontman for two-hit wonder band Moist) also invited them to open for him on a cross-country tour, an offer they declined[13].

More memorable for the band was a gig in New York's Central Park with fellow Canadians Daniel Lanois and Rufus Wainwright—it was a particularly poignant moment for Benvie, being his last show before moving to Toronto, and leaving the band.

Disenchanted with his role as a hired gun, Benvie also found himself butting heads with Lightburn a little too often, probably due to overexposure—he lived on Parc Avenue, right across the street from Lightburn and Yanchak, and had become a fixture at their apartment. "Even though we were friends, we'd just get into stupid arguments," he says. "I'd never really yelled at anyone until I joined The Dears and then I'd be yelling all the time, and it just made me anxious."

That said, Benvie regrets having quit the band the way he did, in the heat of an argument with Lightburn, during the Matthew Good tour. "I basically said, 'I'm planning on quitting this shitty band anyway.' I was a dick about it—I should've waited till the end of the tour. We'd become good friends despite all the bickering, and the other guys—I didn't realize that they would be so sad to see me go. I kind of assumed that they just thought I was hired help."

In hindsight, Benvie acknowledges that he lacked the vision that the rest of the band seemed to have. Despite the

---

13 Good and Usher are effectively MIA in 2011, but you may have heard of two bands who opened for The Dears in 2003: Arcade Fire and Broken Social Scene.

setbacks they'd faced, "there was a feeling that if they kept at it, good things were gonna happen. It's really something that I admire about Murray and Natalia, that they have a lofty vision and they follow through on it."

And sure enough, not long after Benvie's exit, "things started to blow up."

"The tours that I did weren't very romantic, but if I'd stuck around, I probably would've had more fun. I was living in Toronto, working a crappy job, and I'd get these emails from Murray, like, 'Oh, I can't deal with the German press,' and I was just like, 'Fuck you, buddy, enjoy it while you have it.' Obviously, everything's constantly ruining Murray's life, but if worrying about where to eat in Belgium is the worst of your concerns, count yourself lucky."

Patrick Krief started learning guitar at the age of three, and playing blues bars by 13, thanks to his uncles; one of them played guitar, while the other worked as a lighting and sound engineer for rock bands. Initially inspired by virtuoso players like Steve Vai, his methods changed when he began to write his own material at the age of 14.

"I totally went through that phase of playing as if you're getting paid per note," says Krief. "I'm glad I did 'cause it brought some dexterity that comes in handy once in a while. Musically, though, it's gibberish. When I got into songwriting, I pretty much gave up guitar wanking."

In 2003, Krief formed a band to play his solo material, which was modelled on the granddaddies of classic rock and classic pop, from Hendrix to The Beatles. As his drummer, he hired George Donoso III. "I knew he was in some other band called The Dears, but I didn't really know anything about them," says Krief. "Murray and Martin started showing up at a lot of my shows, and Murray would always come talk to me afterwards and be like, 'Oh, you gotta teach me how to play guitar like that.'"

Krief later discovered that he was being "cased" by the band, who were temporarily filling the void left by Benvie with their tour manager and sometimes sound engineer Joseph Donovan. Krief's commitments to school and work removed him from contention for a short time, but after having drifted from film to mathematics to culinary school to finance at a succession of colleges and universities, he brought his academic adventures to an end.

"One night, I told George I'd dropped out and he was just like, right away, 'You wanna join The Dears?' Two days later, I was in the band."

Given Krief's musical leanings and background as a guitarist, his integration into the band wasn't without adjustment and compromise. "It was weird because they're from a completely different school than I was. The things they thought were cool weren't things I knew about or necessarily liked, and some of the stuff I was into was considered not cool. It was weird at first to bring my style of playing into the band 'cause it was hit and miss. Eventually, both sides, my side and the band, leaned into each other and found a spot where we all locked."

Krief's first shows with the band, in March of 2004, coincided with the start of what Yanchak describes as "a whirlwind period." After an eight-date run of shows with Stars that took them from Seattle to Denver, The Dears played several sets at the South by Southwest (SXSW) festival in Austin, Texas. One of these performances caught the attention of Simon Raymonde, co-founder of the Cocteau Twins and head of the U.K. label Bella Union. On his way back to his hotel one night, dejected by the procession of "ordinary" bands he'd seen thus far, Raymonde pushed himself to see one last act, stumbling upon The Dears' set at Buffalo Billiards.

"I kinda knew even as I was walking up the stairs and could hear the huge sound and this amazing voice that I was in the right place," he says. "A few minutes later, I saw the entire U.K. music industry packed in this room and figured the band must already be signed to some big label and this was their album launch party or something. I asked a friend watching if they were signed and he said no."

Attracted by "the energy, the songs, the style, the drama, the charisma, the timing," Raymonde brought The Dears to London for a pair of shows in May of 2004—among the curious onlookers was Blur bassist Alex James—and released *No Cities Left* in the U.K. and Europe in the fall. Critics were predominantly positive, but not unanimous. In Britain, *NME* chose both "We Can Have It" and "Lost in the Plot" as Tracks of the Week, dubbing The Dears "probably the best new band in the world right now." *Q* magazine, who may have accidentally gotten their hands on a copy of *Nor the Dahlias*, commented that the record "can be summed up succinctly: Damon Albarn sings The Smiths."

A similar divide was seen among critics in the U.S., where the band had inked a deal with spinART after SXSW. *Rolling Stone* chose The Dears as one of its "bands to watch" and

Spin gushed, "There isn't a tune on *No Cities Left*, The Dears' gorgeous second album, that's not pitched at a minor state of emergency." The then-increasingly influential music site Pitchfork gave the record a passing grade, but derided it as a "dramatic, flower-throwing, cheekily campy pop record British people were making between the day Morrissey went solo and the day Oasis hit U.S. radio." (Had "Don't Lose the Faith" been included on the American edition, perhaps the writer would've been kind enough to call them Smiths copyists rather than referencing Morrissey's 1991 stinker, *Kill Uncle*.)

But these comparisons didn't particularly hurt The Dears in the U.K., where they went out on a successful 15-date tour. Once home, they played a low-key show at the Pop Montreal festival, and announced some exciting news: in just under two weeks, they would open for Morrissey at Toronto's Hummingbird Centre, as well as L.A.'s Hyundai Pavilion to an estimated 30,000 people on Halloween—Morrissey wore a Catholic priest costume for the occasion.

In a dispatch from the road written months later, Lightburn described meeting his idol in Toronto: "In tears, I shake Morrissey's hand backstage. He basically reminds me to use the force. Those aren't his exact words, but you get the picture."

The Dears wrapped 2004 with 22 U.S. dates and their first tour of Europe, where they played a dozen stages in five countries. Just before Christmas, they returned home triumphant, playing a pair of shows at the intimate La Sala Rossa. Days earlier, local francophone cultural weekly *Voir* had published a Dears article suggesting that the band was at the forefront of a local musical movement. Lightburn said that although he'd recently observed that most Spaniards still viewed Canada as the land of Bryan Adams, Montreal might have a shot at hot spot status.

"I'm not the patriotic type, but what makes this city special is that it's a great place for artists" he said. "I think it's a question of timing; after Seattle, New York and Sweden, maybe it's Montreal's turn?"

CHAPTER 5

We are feeling so erroneously unknown

"You don't have to be a black guy to relate to 'Whites Only Party.' There's always a situation that leaves you feeling a little excluded, where you're banging on the door trying to get into something, and for whatever reason, your face or your shoes or your hair, you're not allowed in."

WHEN THE MONTREAL MUSIC SCENE was thrust into the spotlight in early 2005, The Dears were on their first world tour. It began in the U.K., where 15 of their 20 shows sold out, thanks in part to some heavy press. For Lightburn, it's a fond memory from a time when the band was starting to feel fatigued, itching to get back to the studio but obligated to stay on the road to support a two-year-old album.

"Somebody picks up the *NME* and opens up the middle section and there's like these four animated pictures of me and this huge article," he recalls. "I somehow wound up on their list of the 50 most cool people, I was like #49 or something (laughs), just made it in there. I didn't know how to deal with it at all."

Even more mind-blowing news came down the wire a couple of weeks later, in Brussels, when Yanchak discovered that she was pregnant. The happy couple made the announcement to the rest of the band two weeks later, in Australia.

"Murray was telling it to me like it was bad news," says Krief, "not that he thought it was bad news, but he thought it would let me down or something. He said, 'We're gonna have to take a break,' and I was like 'Oh, thank God.' We'd done 300 shows in a year; the idea of time off was so relieving."

But that respite only came four months later, after two lengthy American tours—including another four sets at SXSW and 16 dates with Sweden's muumuu-wearing widescreen rockers Soundtrack of Our Lives—short jaunts to Europe and the U.K., a 48-hour Canadian-band clusterfuck in Japan (where they shared the stage with Stars, Metric, Broken Social Scene and Death From Above 1979), and a handful of summer festivals in the U.K., Canada and the U.S.

In his 2005 dispatch, written a week before their return, and their biggest local show to date at the Spectrum, Lightburn summed up the festival dates:

"We face off with New Order in Hyde Park. I stand in a foot of mud watching over 100,000 people singing along with Coldplay at Glastonbury. I meet Thurston Moore at Roskilde—screw guitars, let's talk babies. He gives me some valuable advice I'll never forget. Our bus leaves the site while Black Sabbath play a medley of their classics. I witness the NIN comeback in Belgium. They are unbelievable. Really.

We hang out with Interpol and Bloc Party (their singer is black too!) while Rammstein breathes fire in front of over 100,000 people. At T in the Park in Scotland, we park next to Pete Townshend's camper. Yes. The guitarist/writer from The Who is standing right next to our bus. Everyone rushes for their cameras while he turns into a puff of smoke. Perfect. At this point, we have played to thousands and thousands of people and it just doesn't sink in. We count the gigs, days, hours left until we're home. No airports or flights, no buses or vans, no skanks, no ridiculous amounts of booze, no shitty food, no suitcases, no bureaus de change, no immigration, no countries—uh, no cities left. Thank heaven. A really pivotal chapter in Dears history is written. However, there's still so much more to come, and I have zero fear."

During that tour, Lightburn also succumbed to his tendency to give depressive, overly revealing interviews. Fuelled by Stella Artois, he spoke to a reporter from *The Independent*, who titled the article "Big mouth strikes again," about being slandered with accusations of arrogance and egomania in the British press, which he also admonished for putting too much emphasis on the band's Smiths influence. (He'd recently been quoted on the cover of an Australian magazine as saying "If Morrissey is God, I'm Jesus," a joke that was taken seriously.) Back in '03, when the band was touring with Matthew Good, there'd been a similar "train wreck" of an interview on MuchMusic, one that, Lightburn theorized, may have doused the last of the "heat" that the band still had in Toronto. "I heard that people were watching from their offices, and it was just like, 'Oh my God, this is terrible. That's it, it's over for this guy.'" And again, his mood had plummeted just prior to the interview due to bad press, in this case negative reviews of *No Cities Left*. "I didn't know how to process it at all. I was particularly sensitive about that because I had really, really worked my ass off on that album."

Once home, Lightburn's mood was more upbeat, as most of his time was spent being a practical father-to-be, and a prolific musician. After he and Yanchak bought a house in the East Indian/Greek neighbourhood of Park Extension, a fixer-upper with a basement large enough to accommodate a studio, The Dears' third album was underway.

"I was super excited about what Murray was going to come up with," Raymonde says. "He was building a studio and there was a genuine feeling between us that this next record could be a classic work—his songs just seemed to be getting better and better."

In the *Independent* piece, Lightburn hinted that his new lyrics would deal more directly with social issues, specifically the "subtle racism" he'd endured as a touring musician. This had been on his mind as far back as 2003.

"I swear to God, the next journalist who compares me to Sly Stone or Jimi Hendrix or Bob Marley—it's been done, trust me, any black guy with a guitar, singing—I will find them and kick them in the teeth. It just makes me ill. And ever since I started carrying a guitar case, I get, 'Hey, you play bass? You like R&B? You like hip hop?'"

"The black Morrissey" handle, which started spreading up and down music media in '03, was one that Yanchak viewed as an easy way out of addressing Lightburn's ethnicity, and the fact that he's a black guy in a "white" musical realm.

Lightburn took pride in the band's mixed heritage: "George moved here from Chile when he was nine, Martin is as Quebec as it gets, *au boutte*, Natalia is a Pollack/Ukrainian from a Pollack area of Toronto, Valérie is half American, Benvie is a straight-up Canadian white guy and I'm the son of immigrants from Central America," he said. (For the record, Krief is a Jew with roots in Morocco.)

"This is about something bigger than being black or being from fuckin' Quebec or growing up in a Pentecostal church," Lightburn added. "In an ideal world—and we're so far from that—it would be nice to be able to transcend all that bullshit and just be."

The song "Whites Only Party" is an anomaly for The Dears, musically as well as thematically: it's light on guitars and synths and high on rockabilly bounce, reminiscent of Morrissey songs like "Sing Your Life" and "Sister I'm a Poet", with a narrative about the black glass ceiling, inspired by a series of life experiences, but sparked by something specific.

"I'd rather not say exactly what it was, it's a bit on the personal side," Lightburn says. "The thing about that song and the way I write is that it comes from an intensely personal place, but it's meant to be interpreted any which way."

Another influence on Lightburn's lyrics—which amplified the "big love" of *No Cities Left* and moved the magnifying glass from his own troubled heart to that of his society, or at least juxtaposed the two—was the impending arrival of his child. On September 10, 2005, Lightburn and Yanchak were married in a no-frills civil ceremony at the Palais de Justice, with only their parents and band mates in attendance (minus Donoso, who was too hungover to attend). Twenty days later, Yanchak gave birth to a girl, who they named in typical rock star fashion: Neptune Rosita Ursula Yanchak Lightburn—"Neptune" because she's "out of this world."

"A lot of the album was conceived on tour, and when Natalia got pregnant, that factored into things a little bit—how the world will affect [Neptune], how she will affect the world, and what I can do to make it a positive experience.

"But I think our travels around the world made the biggest impact, especially gauging the levels of fearfulness and fearlessness in different places. Fear plays such a huge role in our lives now, and a lot of our outlook involves facing those fears head-on and dismantling them. That's what the whole 'gang of losers' thing is about."

———

Gang of Losers? The album title was derived from a Benvie-ism, which he described as "an affectionate nickname I coined for a certain band with whom we socialized/butted heads." Lightburn expanded on the idea, branding The Dears and their fans as a network of outsiders, in a way that fuses pride and self-deprecation—he'd told *The Independent* in '05 that his fans were "losers" and he was "head geek."

Contrary to the concept, the band appeared to be at the height of their power. They'd signed a new deal for Europe and the U.K., retaining Bella Union as their label but shifting the marketing and distribution duties "upstream" to V2. Three months prior to the record's release, Lightburn did a media blitz across Europe, speaking to reporters for 10 hours a day. In London, however, there were only three interviews booked. One of them was with the *NME*'s Tim Jonze (now a music critic at *The Guardian*), the journalist who, a year later, wrote the infamous article that compared Morrissey's (allegedly?) anti-immigrant views to that of the right-wing extremist British National Party. Lightburn recalls his discomfort during the interview.

"Buddy's asking some pretty fucked up questions, eventually trying to get me to shit-talk Arcade Fire. I started to get paranoid and really cagey, careful. My brain turned into a pretzel, trying to solve a Rubik's Cube with a gun to my head. I went back to my hotel and had a total meltdown. Suddenly, the weight of the pressure, 10 days straight of press, stress and jetlag—suffocating, alone. I felt like, if the [album] was a failure, I was gonna get blamed. Anyway, they never printed that interview, and I wasn't surprised at all."

The *NME* didn't review *Gang of Losers* when it was released, or the record after that. But the reviews that it did receive overseas were largely positive, with the exception of barely passing grades from *Q*, *Blender* and the BBC Collective. There were five stars from *The Guardian*, and four from *Uncut* and *Mojo*. Stateside, it was a mixed bag: they had a cheering section at The Onion A.V., *Spin* and *Under the Radar*, but four thumbs down from Pitchfork, who wrote that poverty and racism are "bigger issues than The Dears are equipped to deal with." Lightburn later retorted: "Clearly that person is either out to sabotage us or they really don't know anything about the band at all. One of the many misconceptions that people have about The Dears is that we've had it easy, so they need to take us down, which is something that Pitchfork does."

Even unanimous acclaim couldn't have made superstars of The Dears in the U.S., but such aspirations weren't unreasonable overseas, where Canadian artists like Feist, Peaches, Danko Jones and Hawksley Workman had had hits. But it soon became clear that the band's attempt to ascend the ranks from indie buzz band to mainstream hitmakers, in the U.K. and Europe, had failed. Sales were lower than expected, partly due to the rise of illegal downloading (the album leaked two months prior to its release), and the buzz that they'd left in the wake of *No Cities Left* had quieted to a faint murmur. Lightburn sees it as an issue of bad timing, missteps on the part of the label and publicist, in their choice of singles and ability to whip up a media frenzy, and the band itself. Both Krief and Donoso had put a foot in it during interviews ahead of the record's release, the former slamming Morrissey's behaviour when the band had opened for him the previous year ("Being asked to leave the building when he's crossing the corridor, or being told to not look directly at him made me sick!"), the latter slamming Toronto's Virgin festival (which, like V2 Records, is a Richard Branson endeavour) as "by far the darkest, cheapest and most ghetto festival ever." Raymonde, who promptly dropped the band, blamed the record's mixed reception on Scott Harding's mix.

"*Gang of Losers*, with its extreme expectations, seemed like a complete disaster at the time," Lightburn says. "And of course the blame game followed, across the board. Everyone was served up a heaping plate of dung and forced to eat it. And everyone was dishing it too."

In retrospect, Lightburn feels that the band should've spent more time on the record and more downtime prior to its recording, admitting that "it was really easy, in hindsight maybe almost too easy, to make." But that's not to say he wasn't proud of the outcome.

Where *No Cities Left* was largely rendered in tight, sharp focus, much of *Gang of Losers* appears in a gauzy longshot, its soaring melodies and universal scope propelled by a lush, sometimes ferocious sonic force. It's hard not to be impressed by the grandeur of "Ticket to Immortality" and "Hate Then Love", yet both songs seem bogged down by arena homogeneity; "Death or Life We Want You" will satisfy a hunger for heavy, but personally, I've never had a taste for grunge; honestly, I didn't even load the first four tracks of *Gang of Losers* onto my MP3 player until I started writing this book. For me, "There Goes My Outfit" is where the record takes off, with Lightburn's impassioned screed backed by those gorgeous "nah-nah-nahs." "Bandwagoneers" is just as compelling, its insistent piano, guitars and decorous keys matching Lightburn's delivery of the song's central thought, "I'm trying to remember when he had control, when we let it…GO-OH-OH!"

"Fear Made the World Go Round" slows and strips proceedings down to a beautiful, if chilling evocation of living beside violence and under fear. Its ethereal blend of piano, keys and reverb-laden vocals accelerates with rough guitars that give way to a swaddling coda where Lightburn coos "we're all okay." In a similar vein, minus the *fromage* finale, the album's last two tracks, "I Fell Deep" and "Find Our Way to Freedom" rely on little window dressing, riding on thin guitars, background synths, rhythm and soul. For the album's climax, Lightburn's father cameos on sax, sealing a lyrically dramatic yet sonically understated track with some showy brass. With its arpeggiated rhythms and bobbing melodies, "Freedom" is rather reminiscent of Radiohead, but alongside "Fear" and "Fell", present a progressive shift for the band.

———————

I cried the first time I heard "You and I Are a Gang of Losers", live at the Spectrum. Only a minute in, something about the slowly gathering steam of the piano, keys, drums and guitar (in that order), and Lightburn's first utterance of the mantra "You and I are on the outside of almost everything," set up the waterworks, which spill as soon as he and Yanchak duet on the big line "cos we, we've got the same haw-aw-aw-art"— that four-step descending melody is just KILLER. Actually, I'm tearing up right now.

Gang of Losers is widely considered to be The Dears' high water mark. In industry circles, this could be based on little more than the band's visibility peaking during that album cycle, with their appearance on *Letterman* and their nomination for the inaugural Polaris Prize in Canada. Among serious fans, there's stiff competition from *No Cities Left*, the album that perfected the band's "orchestral pop noir romantique." But *Losers* is a monumental game changer, as important, and nearly as strong, as such classic career-transitioning albums as Bowie's *Station to Station* or Radiohead's *OK Computer*. As Lightburn told Montreal's daily English newspaper, *The Gazette*, "(The sound) is a result of us wanting to reinvent ourselves. We wanted to push the band forward. It was six people making as much noise as they can."

CHAPTER 6

See I've come back from almost death

"It could've died, and I wasn't ready to let it die.
For me to continue, it was either, I'm making an album
by myself or I'm hijacking the band back, and that's
essentially what I've had to do is take back the band."

MONTHS BEFORE *Gang of Losers* hit the streets—between August and October 2006, depending on the region—the band returned to the road, Neptune in tow, for another lengthy stretch, from April 2006 to July 2007, with intervals every month or two. The strain that every touring band feels, given the close quarters, gruelling schedules, questionable diet and heavy drinking, was exacerbated for The Dears by a growing rift between the two couples.

In early August 2006, Benvie travelled to Sorel-Tracy, Quebec, to attend the wedding of "the Frenches" (an in-house term of endearment for Pelland and Jodoin-Keaton, the Québécois couple). He remembers the "dispirited look" in the eyes of Lightburn and Yanchak, who began to confide in him as relations turned sour. That was the last time he saw the couples together.

"There was definitely a slow crumbling of our friendship," says Yanchak. "We weren't communicating with each other in a meaningful way. We just started going through the motions."

Though there was certainly a personal element to the Frenches' disenchantment with Lightburn and Yanchak, the root of the problem, as Yanchak sees it, was money. During the *No Cities Left* period, Lightburn had made a publishing deal that put the band in the black for the first time. Though he wasn't legally required to share the money, which, as the band's songwriter, arranger and producer, was rightly his, not to mention the fact that he and Yanchak had spent nearly every waking hour prior to Neptune's birth dealing with "rock 'n' roll business," he split an undisclosed percentage of the money between the other members (minus Krief, who opted to remain a "hired gun"), creating a partnership that essentially paid them a salary. But by 2007, it wasn't enough and tensions mounted.

Yanchak describes the disintegration of the band as "fucking hell—I wouldn't wish that kind of shit on anyone.

"After *Gang of Losers* wasn't as successful as *No Cities Left* had been, I think everyone started to panic, and instead of taking a break, we just kept touring. It all started to fall apart but no one had any time to think about what the fuck was going on."

Krief found himself in an awkward, albeit neutral position. As the newest addition to the band, and one who didn't even regard himself as a permanent member, given the impending release of a record by his own band, Black Diamond Bay (in which Donoso was still the drummer), he was the go-to ear and shoulder. "I was like a kid in the middle of a divorce," he says. "Everybody felt safe telling me what they felt. They wouldn't communicate with each other but I would get a full dose of it from each team."

What was transpiring behind the scenes, according to Yanchak, came down to Pelland and Jodoin-Keaton wanting to explore only the most lucrative options for the band. Donoso typically sided with them—when the band was discussing the possibility of building a small tour around a show they'd been offered in Istanbul, he said that he could make more money DJing in Montreal.

"That vision that we lived for was being pulled in all these directions," Yanchak says. "Maybe it's my fault or Murray's fault or us as a team being so dedicated to it that we didn't want to see it diluted for the wrong reasons.

"[The band members] were talking for hours and hours and we just weren't understanding each other. We were on different planes. [Murray and I] realized that we didn't know these people anymore, maybe we never did. They were asking us to compromise everything that we'd worked for and to put it at the mercy of money, so that money would be the only reason for us to continue working on this project, and that was really hard for us."

Finally, in late August of 2007, Pelland and Jodoin-Keaton were "asked to leave."

"I think it took them a while to accept what had happened," Krief opines. "I don't think they appreciated, after all the years that they'd been involved, not having had an option to work things out—they did make efforts at the 11th hour, which may or may not have been too late."

Although he stuck around to record drum parts for the next record, Donoso ultimately followed Jodoin-Keaton and Pelland out the door. Together, they formed a short-lived band called For Those About to Love, releasing an eponymous album in 2009.

Donoso's departure came as a shock to Krief, who was already halfway out the door himself, shifting his attention to Black Diamond Bay. "He kind of gave us the strength to move forward without Martin and Val," Krief says. "It was shitty for me 'cause I had already told Murray that I might leave, and when George pulled that curveball, it was like, 'Oh shit, how am I gonna lay it on Murray now?' I thought he at least had his anchor."

"Musically, I always had a blast with Murray, and I miss that—I miss making music with him," Donoso says. "Till about 2005, we had this beautiful friendship, this beautiful family vibe, and that magic kinda disappeared and turned into business and drama."

Donoso's primary reason for quitting was the lack of democracy in the band. He resented, for example, Lightburn's refusal to pursue corporate gigs, and his decision to record *Gang of Losers* in his home studio—Donoso feels that that record "just doesn't sound right," as a result. But ultimately, he felt the need to regain control of his life and move on. He's currently the drummer with another quality Montreal band, The High Dials.

Krief is evidently on side with Lightburn and Yanchak, yet he regrets that there was no attempt to repair the fracture.

"I really feel like the whole thing could've been prevented if we'd had proper intervention from management," says Krief. "I mean, you see bands that have it so much worse, people that hate each other, and I don't think it ever boiled to that point. There were definite bad vibes and trash-talking going on, and a couple dirty moves here and there, but if we'd all sat down with a mediator or group therapist or something, it would've been banged out in a couple sessions."

Mediation was an option that had been considered as far back as Yanchak's pregnancy in 2005. Their management at the time wanted no part of the drama, so they began to look elsewhere. "I was talking to one potential manager," Yanchak recalls, "and getting really emotional, I was pouring my heart out to this guy, and I asked him, 'What would you do if you came on?' and he was like, 'I would get you guys back together.' That probably could have saved us, but other aspects of the way he wanted to roll weren't right for us."

Near the end of 2010, Krief intimated that his feelings about this episode remain unresolved. "Even though the new line-up is unstoppable, I still get annoyed when I think about what went down."

———

Towards the end of The Dears' 2007 tour, with only four dates left before they essentially broke up, they played a show that Lightburn calls an "unforgettable" career highlight, despite being tainted by bittersweetness.

"Just when the band was miserable and hating each other, we went to Mexico and played this sold-out, 1,200-capacity joint. That was the most insane gig I've ever played in my life. When we got off stage and we were about to go back to do an encore, I remember Val coming up to me and trying to hug me, and I was like, 'Are you kidding me?' I was thinking, 'In my mind, I'm already gone. This hug right here is too late.'"

A few months after the band had played their last show together, Lightburn elaborated on his decision:

"Philosophically, I didn't like the direction that the band was headed in. Maybe we could've emerged on another level and maybe everything could've been okay, but the stuff that had gone down was just so unbelievably dark and, in my opinion, pretty irreparable, that I had to make a decision. But it wasn't easy."

———

What was left of the band emerged from the battle wounded, and facing a lengthy recovery. But within weeks of losing "a couple of soldiers," as Lightburn cryptically announced in November of 2007, a new album was in the works.

Creatively, the band was on fire, free to explore new arrangements, techniques and vocal stylings because they felt, as Lightburn said, that they hadn't truly experimented for years, and they had nothing left to lose. After working for five "feverish" weeks at home, he and Yanchak, Krief and Donoso, along with Dears alumni Arquilla and Benvie, took it to Montreal's Studio Plateau and Mountain City, the latter run by their friends Joseph Donovan and onetime Tricky Woo bassist Adrian Popovich. The band's twiddling and tweaking sometimes became excessive. With Krief (aka "the doctor," who could identify and execute guitar ideas with stunning speed), they worked on effects, riffs and solos inspired by blues, funk, grunge and metal. With Benvie, who was briefly dubbed the band's Nick Rhodes (the keyboardist from the early days of Duran Duran), they worked on one keyboard sound for four hours, and set up mics in a stairwell to capture the crashes of runaway percussion.

"Years ago, my old band Thrush Hermit had an album with a budget, and I had this idea that we would throw a glockenspiel down a flight of stairs," says Benvie. But Thrush Hermit was "diehard, often painfully, punk-rock frugal. Excess was against our rules. In The Dears, excess is the name of the game.

"I had this sound in my mind and it seemed to really fit for 'Disclaimer.' So I said, 'I don't really have any ideas for this song, it seems to be pretty done, but we gotta throw a glockenspiel down a flight of stairs,' and we did and it sounded awesome."

―――――――

In the early stages, it wasn't clear whether or not the record that would become *Missiles* would be a Dears release, but Lightburn decided that going solo would've been too "bluesy." Krief, Benvie and Arquilla weren't available to tour when *Missiles* was released in October of 2008, so the band found itself in the same position it had been in eight years earlier: stripped to its nucleus, with a record in the can, in search of new players. They wound up with Pony Up!'s Lisa Smith (bass) and Laura Wills (keys), guitarists Christopher McCarron (of Land of Talk) and Jason Kent (then a solo artist and guitarist for hire, now the leader of Sunfields) and drummer Yann Geoffroy (of Kill the Lights).

"For me, the concept of The Dears is greater than the personnel," Lightburn says, "but that's not to discount the personnel. The personnel is guided into the path of The

Dears for a reason. There's a spirit that inhabits The Dears, and when you become a part of The Dears, you're basically walking into a haunted house, and anything can happen[14]."

As far out as this mythologizing may seem, it appeared to come from a genuine place, as did Lightburn's inclusion of himself among the band's "personnel." While most people view The Dears as Lightburn's "lifework," a project that could never exist without his voice, words and music, he has said that he feels differently. "That's my dream: that The Dears continues even after I'm gone," he says. Though he doesn't want to be "a hockey dad," he can foresee passing the band on to Neptune, who "has been known to sit at a piano or pick up a guitar and actually say, 'I wanna rock.'" But he's also pondered the idea of his mysterious source of inspiration inhabiting another host.

"I wake up in the morning and I hear sounds in my head and I don't know where the sounds come from," he says. Many musicians have wondered whether supernatural or celestial forces are at work when a song just hits them and spills out almost fully formed. In Lightburn's case, the idea of the band outliving him—whether via his daughter or the transference of inspirational spirits—was likely brought on by the brush with mortality that influenced so many of the songs he wrote in 2007. He'd suffered a series of "long, stress-related coughing fits," and the occasional panic attack, including one that ruined the results of a CT scan. "I literally

---

14 Moving from horror to sci-fi metaphors, Lightburn also imagined membership in the band as a vacuum sucking musicians into a portal. "Some people don't even know that that gateway has opened up and that they've been pulled in, and the next thing you know, six, seven years have gone by and you've been a part of this thing."

thought about death and dying every second of the day for months," he says. This morbid outlook is reflected in a series of songs that deal with body horror, while spiritual horror is exorcised on "Saviour", which Lightburn calls his "lone wolf howling at the moon at night" song. Though somewhat restrained vocally, its lyrics and stark arrangement, which builds from a bare beat punctuated by haunting strums to a quasi-gospel climax, capture the emotional repercussions of facing down death, with religious overtones writ large.

"I was on the phone with my mother, in complete meltdown mode," he recalls. "She was praying with me, 'cause that's what she does. After I got off the phone, I went down to my basement and wrote the song."

On top of a piano riff that recalls Julee Cruise's "The World Spins" (as heard in a particularly heavy sequence from *Twin Peaks*), the Every Kid Choir lent the song some extra uplifting, anthemic heft, while the Brébeuf Brass (aka Chris Seligman, Evan Cranley and Matt Watkins), who'd previously appeared on *No Cities Left*, provided the dirge. "My direction to them was to pretend that they were playing at my funeral, eulogizing me. I wanted super-sad horns and they delivered it."

Lightburn admits that a fine line between heaviness and cheesiness may have been crossed on this song, and maybe it was, but the song nevertheless ends the record with the grace and style of a tasteful eulogy with a redemptive underpinning.

Not all of *Missiles* was this dark. The record launches with the brash spirit of "Disclaimer", a lush, catchy concoction of chiming guitars and sax; "Money Babies" is the big pop song, matching a stinging rhythm with melodies and his 'n' hers harmonies so pretty, they could serve as a lullaby, if the lyrics weren't so cynical: "Our money is elastic / gotta get milk for the baby," they say, painting an ugly picture of "cavalcades of losers," disaster, decapitation and death—clearly, this is an allusion to what the *Missiles*-era bio refers to as the "outright mutiny" that had nearly brought down the band. The malaise persists on "Demons", which pairs a snappy, upbeat rhythm with ghostly keyboards and sharp guitar licks. Yanchak takes the lead on the cool, mid-paced pop tune "Crisis 1 & 2", her best turn at centre stage thus far. In fine voice, she sings of hazards and suicide missions, while beautifully choreographed acoustic and electric guitars coil around each other in the dark, some of them slithering backwards; the song transitions and Lightburn injects a little vigour, singing about an approaching train as riffs and rhythm gather steam and surge while he sings, "Oh Lord, yeah I'm talking to you, it's been a life long sentence and you thought we were through, but now I'm dying to know how much you care!"

"Dream Job" stews in its own languid melancholy, as does the two-part song "Lights Off", which begins with a peppy pace, grinds into a guitar explosion and ends with a fallout lullaby. "Berlin Heart" has an even sweeter, rock-a-bye-baby quality, despite its dark lyrical undertones, and a surprising inclusion of a banjo and whistling. "Meltdown in A Major" and the album's title track form a bleak epicentre; the latter's shrill despair recalls "Acoustic Guitar Phase" from the *OPNR* EP, complete with a quivering falsetto and racial epithets. But the climax is eons from acoustic, culminating in Sabbath-esque guitar sludge and an unhinged metal solo.

Having never been a fan of the band's tendency to lose itself in jamming and shredding, or their uncomfortably raw and intimate tangents, this is the *Missiles* song I listen to least. Yet it's still impressive, even next to the record's most sumptuous pop highs and bluesy lows. It's a flawed album, featuring experiments that fail and succeed, one that's fuelled by duress but ultimately elevated by a defiance that you can feel.

It may be difficult to reconcile such songcraft, so personal and steeped in narcissistic melancholia, with the idea that The Dears could be anyone else's baby but Lightburn's—even his own baby's. The thought of the band as a "force" could also come from an egomaniacal place, and yet Lightburn's health scare and the band's tribulations seem to have instilled a fresh and deep humility in him.

"The Dears are in an ideal spot," he said at the time, "because we're just playing our little gigs and putting out our little records. It doesn't have to be about being the biggest, the best, the strongest, the fastest.

"What it is that makes the band what it is, is always gonna be there. That shit is always gonna rain down on The Dears, there's nothing you can do about it. No matter what combination you try to put together, it's gonna come out all fucked up, mangled up, messed up. That's what it's gonna be; trying to be pop music but just not quite getting there," he concluded, laughing.

Lightburn explored the band's philosophy and his conflicting views on being a musician in a series of webisodes that were not so humbly entitled The Gospel According to the Dears. He shot a series of interviews with André Bendahan, who, despite being a member of Black Diamond Bay, was unable to convince his bandmate Donoso to take part, let alone Pelland and Jodin-Keaton.

"In editing this thing, I've learned a lot … about perceptions and assumptions and presumptions," Lightburn said. "The more you put yourself out there, the more you, unfortunately, become aware of yourself, which is really painful. Just yesterday, Laura [Wills] called me a self-hating rock star, because I hate rock stardom but, she said, nonetheless, stop denying it. It made me laugh out loud, but maybe there's some truth to it. On some levels, it's an enjoyable gig, on other levels, it's not enjoyable at all."

Critics were divided in the face of *Missiles*. *Spin* derided the band with the tired old accusation of Smiths worship, which is completely absent on this record; they also slammed the "überwanky guitar solos" on "Lights Off", only spinning positively about two songs. *Prefix* magazine also dealt out a slap-down, simultaneously categorizing the band as U2 wannabes and Britpop revivalists, guilty of "clunky" prose on "Money Babies", which they then absurdly interpret literally. The Dears' old nemeses at Pitchfork rated the record more highly than any previous Dears release, despite dishing out large servings of nitpicking and faint praise. The British critics were positive: *The Guardian* deemed the record "as complex and beautiful as you'd expect from Montreal's grand miserablists," and *Mojo* and *Q* magazine were equally impressed, championing the band's "heartfelt, inventive arrangements" and "intimacy and honesty," respectively.

The Dears began to emerge from what Lightburn called a "teary chapter" once they were back on stage. The new line-up made its hometown debut several weeks prior to the record's release, during Pop Montreal. In a move typical of the festival—whose founder, Dan Seligman (brother of Chris from Stars) is friends with Lightburn and Yanchak—the band was booked at an unconventional venue: the Masonic Memorial Temple. Bathed in blue and red light that beamed from their gear, the band of pros sounded tight, peppering the *Missiles*-heavy set with tunes from *Gang of Losers* and *No Cities Left*. I was surprised to see Donoso in the crowd, bobbing his head to the songs he used to play.

Though the show wasn't terribly animated, on the part of the band and the seated crowd, Lightburn was in good humour, leading a funny, musical introduction of the band deep into the set.

Two weeks later, they flew across the Atlantic for a couple of shows in London, beginning at the baroque Porchester Hall.

"At our first gig in London, people's reaction to the band was just really comforting," Lightburn said, having recently returned from tour. "Playing the shows has been really great to do, just to get out there."

The band got out there 29 times in 2008, almost exclusively in North America. At the end of January 2009, they played another show in Montreal, at St. James United Church. It was a fundraiser for the Every Kid Choir, the band's way of returning a favour for their contribution to "Saviour", which was recorded for free. Over a backing track, they joined Lightburn for a "choral karaoke" rendition of the song. Almost equally memorable were the obnoxious antics of a drunken fan, which escalated from requests for old songs to full-on interruptions during quiet moments, such as the intro to "Lights Off". After Lightburn jokingly offered up his mic, the heckler was dragged out of the room. There were also at least two couples making out in the pews. "We've finally seen it all," Lightburn said.

Sometime in the early months of 2009, bassist Lisa Smith quit the band, and with a six-week North American tour coming up in May, they turned to their alumni to pick up the slack.

"In serendipity, I was just quitting my job, I was just really fed up," Benvie said of his return. "I had this chunk of time before a trip I'd planned to India. It actually fit perfectly. So I was like, yeah, why the hell not? I hadn't been on the road in a while."

The Dears made the news just as their tour was about to begin—in Pointe Claire, a suburb just west of Montreal, their tour bus was stolen from a hotel parking lot. Luckily there was no gear or luggage inside, and they were able to play Toronto as scheduled, on the last day of April. They capped the *Missiles* album cycle with another Toronto show, a free gig at the 2,000-capacity Harbourfront Centre in late July of 2009. But by far the highlight of their year was a pair of dates in Mexico, where they were once again greeted by a rapturous fanbase.

"The Dears' heart was beating slowly and was dying," Lightburn told the Mexican crowd during the show, "but Mexico has injected blood and made it stronger again, beating with more strength than ever. We will never forget this."

CHAPTER 7

We've got to know what happened here, and what the hell we're looking for

"The challenge we always face is achieving some kind of
perfection. Standing at the bottom of the mountain
looking up, wondering how we get from here to there.
We're doing it again because the gods say so. They'll
call us home when our work here is done."

BY THE TIME THE DEARS MADE THEIR WAY BACK to Mexico City
in May of 2010, they'd written 30 new songs. Together.
According to Krief, Lightburn made a game-changing
proposition over drinks at yet another St-Laurent watering
hole Korova back in 2009:

Lightburn How would you feel about writing for The
Dears?

Krief What do you mean?

L When I heard the Black Diamond Bay record, I wish I

had been a part of it.

K Well, I'd love to write with you. For The Dears?

L Yeah, for The Dears.

K I don't know, what are you talking about, co-writing?

L Yeah, I'm talking Lennon/McCartney.

K That's a big one. Let me think about it.

L You need to think about that?

K Yeah.

L What do I have to do, get on my knees and blow you?

It never came to blows, as Krief was as unwilling to turn down the offer (to co-write, that is) as Lightburn was to take no for an answer. Ever since Krief had left the band, many of their conversations culminated in Lightburn applying pressure to rejoin ("We could be talking about *Lost* for an hour, and then it'd be, like, 'When the fuck are you gonna come back to the band?'" Krief said), but opening the door to collaborative songwriting was something new.

In January of 2009, Lightburn half-joked about starting a solo project so as not to "take up too much real estate" in The Dears. He may have already considered co-writing as a way to attract, and retain, the band members he most wanted (the *Missiles* crew, having "served their time admirably," would soon "get an honourable discharge," as Lightburn put it later that year). He suspected that exclusion from the creative process was what had driven some former band members away. And yet he also insisted that The Dears is fundamentally a joint effort.

"People walk away from that collaboration thinking that they were just a hired gun, that they never contributed anything, and I refuse to believe or accept that," he says.

Lightburn and Krief's songwriting partnership was built on a common ability to see an idea through within hours of an inspirational strike; to render a melody, progression and even arrangement into a nearly complete song, in demo form. They fused their respective song ideas, old and new, in one case almost effortlessly pasting one of Krief's stray parts into one of Lightburn's unfinished songs.

"Bam, done!" Lightburn says. "I was blown away by that, but I always kinda knew that we were kindred spirits on that level."

They co-wrote six of the new songs ("5 Chords", "Torches", "Galactic Tides", "Tiny Man", "Easy Suffering", "1854"), while one ("Thrones") was brought to the table by Benvie, who had also been invited back into the fold. During his five years in Toronto, Benvie had published a novel, *The Safety of War*, worked on his solo music project, Tigre Benvie, and played in the electro-funk rock band Camouflage Nights, on top of holding down a day job. By 2009, he had tired of the city and was already considering a move, with a girlfriend who's a native of *la belle province*. The offer to join The Dears in a creative capacity, and not just learn Lightburn's songs, sealed the deal.

"Benvie is a genius on every level," Lightburn states, extolling the virtues of the "crack commando team" that was unleashing "heavy creativity" in the band's rehearsal space. "He's actually too smart. It's annoying."

Though they've since gotten to know each other and made their complementary talents mesh, Benvie initially questioned whether he and Krief would work well together, given their disparate guitar styles and contradictory philosophies. "He's such a great guitarist and I'm kind of a hack. He brings so much passion to it, and he's so neurotic about it, too, 'cause he invests himself in it so deeply. I come from the self-deprecating, ironic grunge era where it's really not cool to toot your own horn and it's really not cool to care, even though I do care."

Initially assigned bass duty, Benvie shifted to synths for the recording—on stage, he sings back-up and plays guitar and a Fender Rhodes electric piano. Stepping in on bass was yet another familiar face, Roberto Arquilla, who'd lent a hand on *Missiles* (bass and mixing) and had stuck close to Lightburn and Yanchak since quitting the band way back in 1998. Since then, he'd briefly played bass with Memphis, the side project of Stars singer Torquil Campbell, but his primary role in the music realm (he's also been a handyman and cook) was sound engineer, for acts such as Stars, Sam Roberts and Bloc Party.

Alongside the all-star line-up is drummer Jeff Luciani, the new guy from St. Catharines, ON, who Lightburn describes as "a heavy dude. He's a very, very intense drummer and an intense guy but he's also really funny, so he fits in perfectly."

From Benvie's perspective, even though he and Lightburn still sometimes butt heads, the band dynamic has improved with the passage of time.

"It's certainly more positive," he says. "I'm probably the biggest asshole in the band now—well, next to Murray. But everybody else is pretty level-headed and agreeable."

With a crew so tight and in tune with each other, the creation of the latest record, *Degeneration Street*, was remarkably smooth and drama-free.

"It was all business," Lightburn reports, "just us in a room, stinking it up, hashing out songs and beating the shit out of them until they were as perfect as we could conceive."

"All the songs bear everyone's stamp," Benvie explains, "but in the end, Murray *is* The Dears—it's still Murray's voice and Murray's lyrics and Murray's vision—but there's room for others to play a role in it. It works because everybody understands that."

The one person who superseded Lightburn in the studio was Tony Hoffer, the acclaimed producer who's worked with the likes of Beck, Belle and Sebastian, Goldfrapp and Phoenix. And with his help, and that of engineer David Schiffman, The Dears got the results they were looking for. "Sonically, it's the best thing we've ever done," Lightburn states.

———

Degeneration Street was released in February and March of 2011 by Dangerbird in the U.S., U.K. and Europe. In Canada, the band has a new deal with Pheromone, a label founded by Kim Cooke, the same man who signed the band to MapleMusic in 2002. His opinion is hardly objective, but Cooke feels that this is the band's best work, and I'm tempted to agree.

Throughout the record's conception and production, Lightburn talked about "making a record that is super tough and hard as nails," with elements of glam rock, hip hop and "sci-fi-grunge," and "undeniable, fist-pumping tunes," "mellow and pretty" material and a "dark side" that's "stewing in its own rage." He also forecast the return of orchestral, baroque and symphonic features, supplied by the usual brass suspects Chris Seligman and Evan Cranley, along with The Stills' Liam O'Neill and a hired string quartet.

Nearly all of these elements are woven into the album's hypnotic opener, "Omega Dog". Over a distinctly Dears synth wheeze, Luciani drops some sweet rolls and a beat fitted with wide grooves that are promptly filled with a snarky guitar riff. Lightburn arrives in a striking falsetto, with minimal lyrics that don't make a lot of sense, but sound great regardless. The song shifts midway to more familiar Dears territory: a soft, spiralling guitar riff is gradually piled with synth, organ, escalating drums, a mantra ("I'm the only one"), violin, harpsichord and a second guitar that whips into a frenzy, abetted by sci-fi SFX and calamitous crashes.

Banging drums and guitars signal the start of "5 Chords", a booming, insistent rocker with incongruously sentimental lyrics, couched in a feeling of impending doom. Conversely, "Blood" begins innocently enough, with a bobbing riff and harpsichord, before bursting into a sleazy, raucous groove, paired with a sinister screed—on *Missiles* "Disclaimer", Lightburn sings, "I wanna pummel some heads," but here his command "bring all their heads to me" feels more sincere. And awesome.

The windswept melodies and monumental guitars and keys of Benvie's song "Thrones" is strangely reminiscent of some of The Manic Street Preachers' maxed out arena rockers, in the best possible way. And this is where the band takes it down, with the graceful elegy "Lamentation". From Yanchak's ghostly coos (one of only two minor vocal showcases she has on this record), the song gives way to a loud, thorny centre that culminates in the soaring cries of what sounds like a choir, but is actually two members of the Montreal roots band

Ladies of the Canyon. This segues into the orchestral sci-fi instrumental, "Torches", which eases us into "Galactic Tides", a reverb-soaked chamber-rocker that re-introduces the two-member choir, and a beautiful vision of the apocalypse. The climax squeals, screams and soars with fitting finality.

Snap out of that foetal position and grab a partner for "Yesteryear", a swing-time cousin of "Whites Only Party" that evokes vintage Motown more than Morrissey (if Motown had rocked harpsichords and pummelling noise). That momentum carries over into "Stick w/ Me Kid", a song fuelled by an urgency that chugs aggressively through the verses, riding on violins and guitars, and roars into overdrive in the noisy chorus: "I will run till there's nowhere left to run! I will love till there's no one left to love!"

Though the pace abates over the remainder of the record, each song is imbued by a distinct passion: "Tiny Man" is melancholy, minor-key drama with glammy décor, and an alluring, mysterious chorus; "Easy Suffering" is an inspirational pop-rocker that's nearly fit for radio, or your local arena, despite the dearth of big clichés; the relatively minimal, Radiohead-esque "Unsung" sounds, musically and lyrically, like the optimistic inverse of "Find Our Way to Freedom" (which was also the 12th track, two albums back). With "1854", the record returns to dark terrain, though perhaps not as dark as you might think—Lightburn denied that the title is a reference to American history (or Oscar Wilde, for that matter). But the album's title track hits the true depths of bleakness, proving that this is an album of extremes. Take the smartest, most emotionally stirring post-apocalyptic sci-fi, cross it with Joy Division's "Decades", toss in some medieval partying, self-flagellation and an expiring soul howling at the moon, and you may approximate the feeling of "Degeneration Street". It's no wonder that this song's title was chosen to represent the album. Both are works of staggering, gripping beauty, earthly to a fault but effortlessly ethereal all the same.

In the fall of 2010, The Dears played *Degeneration Street* live, in its entirety and in its running order, at a series of three-night residencies. When I spoke to Lightburn over espresso at a fancy Park Ex bakery that September, the band was in the midst of "serious bootcamp" in preparation for their hometown run, in the basement of the Mission Santa Cruz Church, a Portuguese establishment in the Plateau. They were "rehearsing like motherfuckers, six hours a day, five or six days a week" to perfect the set that they'd performed four months earlier, over those three nights in Mexico City.

"It was such an awesome feeling," Lightburn reported. "Terrifying, challenging, for us and the audience 'cause they'd never heard a note of it."

Fans around the world heard "Omega Dog" for the first time via a professionally filmed live clip from one of the Mexican shows, which hit the internet in the fall. The clip, and the others from the same shows that have emerged since, captures the strength of the new line-up and the famous fervour of the Mexican fans, some of whom partied with the band after one of the shows.

Logistically challenging, technically nightmarish ("It was gong show," as Lightburn put it), the residency experiment was a success. Momentum built from the time the band touched down in Mexico: a couple dozen reporters showed up at their press conference, helping to spread the word about the series of shows at Pasaguero, a 300-capacity venue that packed in more and more people each night. The crowd at the third and final show, according to Lightburn, was 600-strong. "I don't know how they did it, it was scary at times."

The impetus for the residencies, which also took place in October and November in Toronto and Brooklyn, N.Y., was partly to "set up camp," "plant roots" and "build something."

"Because the show is so fleeting, you want to give people the chance to see it more than once and you want as many people to see it as possible," Lightburn says. "It's kind of like the circus is coming to town for three days."

Playing the record from top to bottom was a treat for fanbases in each city, and served as a series of dress rehearsals/warm-up shows for the band, as well as a novelty to attract media attention.

Such a presentation isn't exactly unheard of—in recent years, the likes of Public Enemy and The Charlatans have performed their classic albums in their entirety—but not many bands push new material this way, certainly not months prior to a record's release. It was a risky move that could've alienated casual Dears connoisseurs (though the encores were packed with oldies), but Lightburn saw it as a way to revive a feeling of fanticipation that the internet has helped to destroy.

"That excitement over hearing a new song and [then] going out to buy the record is finished," Lightburn says, nostalgically recalling the way he used to preview and procure new music, via alternative radio shows and underground record stores. "Part of our mandate now is to try and recreate that while engaging in this new age. Doing these shows is only scratching the surface of how we see things going down for us in the future."

Three months prior to the release of *Degeneration Street*, the band began hosting weekly webcasts live from their basement studio, wherein they'd play their classics, deep cuts, videos, demos and other unreleased material, chat about random Dears-related topics (such as this book) and reveal one new song per week, while fans from all over the world logged in and chatted away. It was another gift for the "diehards," and a good time for the band.

"For a couple of years, being in The Dears was not fun at all," Lightburn admits, "but it's fun to me again, it's fun to all of us again."

———————

Over a decade in, having achieved modest success, with real rock stardom ever out of reach, The Dears could be viewed as a pack of musicians simply working a job. Many other bands in the same position are doing just that. But for Lightburn, there are no other options because making music isn't a career, it's a compulsion.

"When you wake up in the morning and you have to sit at the piano and get this fucking piece of shit out of your head, when you're at that level of making art, whether it's sitting at a piano or splashing paint on a canvas or carving out some stone, chances are you're gonna do that till you die."

Benvie also recognizes that what drives The Dears isn't the adoration, let alone the money. It's simply "what you do."

"I sort of feel like being 35 years old and still playing in a rock band is not very dignified," he says, "but when you find your vocation, you pursue it as best you can."

In a Mexican TV interview, taped during the 2010 Mexico City residency, Benvie opined that The Dears is more than just a vocation, or just a band: "Sometimes it's a family, or sometimes it's an art project, sometimes it feels like it's a political cause that's been swept up and we're all getting carried away and next thing you know, we're out playing shows and it's like, 'How did this happen?' Well, we launched this revolution and now we have to back it up, so we have to put our...not money...we have to put our music where our mouths are."

Back in 2003, Yanchak rebuffed the idea that the band employs a cult of personality, or values rock stardom: "Fuck, we'll play behind a curtain, it doesn't matter," she said. "Unfortunately, that's part of marketing an album, using people. But at the end of the day, you don't go home with the people. You go home with the music."

And if music is the barometer of life for the band, the renewed vigour and ne plus ultra quality of *Degeneration Street* gives credence to Lightburn's claim that The Dears have hit a restart button, and just might "make new works every couple of years for the rest of time."

"This is how I felt around [the time of] *End of a Hollywood Bedtime Story*," he said in September of 2010, "that feeling of having something to prove.

"Nobody else really cares, but I think it's an amazing story: you start a band, you have some success, you take a few things for granted, then you have a meltdown and then you start over again—and yet we're still The Dears. And we're hardly done. We're just getting started."

THE BIBLIOPHONIC SERIES is a
catalogue of the ongoing history of
contemporary music. Each book
is a time capsule, capturing artists
and their work as we see them,
providing a unique look at some of
today's most exciting musicians.

Invisible Publishing
Halifax & Toronto